I'M AN AMERICAN

A PERSONAL APPROACH TO EARLY AMERICAN HISTORY

Written by
Bruce Olav Solheim, Ph.D.

Illustrations by
Gary Dumm

I'm An American: A Personal Approach to Early American History

Copyright 2024 © Bruce Olav Solheim, Ph.D.

Written by Bruce Olav Solheim, Ph.D.
Illustrations by Gary Dumm
Edited by George Verongos

This is the sole work of the author, and no portion of this publication may be copied or re-published in any publication without express permission of the publisher or author.

ISBN: 9798218495824

Boots to Books
Glendora, CA 91741 USA
bootstobooks@gmail.com
www.bruceolavsolheim.com

Dedication and Thanks

This *anti-textbook* is dedicated to all students of history, young and old. I would like to thank my family, my friends, my colleagues, and my students. I would also like to thank my illustrator and friend, Gary Dumm. Lastly, I would like to thank my editor and friend, George Verongos.

Content

INTRODUCTION: Defining America 1

CHAPTER ONE COMIC: Gentle Giants 4

CHAPTER ONE: Initiating America 5

CHAPTER TWO COMIC: Leif the Lucky .... **Error! Bookmark not defined.**

CHAPTER TWO: Discovering America 27

CHAPTER THREE COMIC: The 1526 Project 40

CHAPTER THREE: Colonizing America 41

CHAPTER FOUR COMIC: Crispus Attacked! 62

CHAPTER FOUR: Revolutionizing America 63

CHAPTER FIVE COMIC: Big Ben & Elizabeth 82

CHAPTER FIVE: Founding America 83

CHAPTER SIX COMIC: Old Hickory 106

CHAPTER SIX: Building America 107

CHAPTER SEVEN COMIC: Rapper's Delight 122

CHAPTER SEVEN: Reforming America 123

CHAPTER EIGHT COMIC: Charleston Choose 144

CHAPTER EIGHT: Dividing America 145

CONCLUSION: Claiming America 163

Index 165

About the Author 169

INTRODUCTION

Defining America

"Citizens by birth or choice, of a common country, that country has a right to concentrate your affections. The name of American, which belongs to you, in your national capacity, must always exalt the just pride of Patriotism, more than any appellation derived from local discriminations."

—*George Washington (1796)*

I did not want to write another history book because I was nearing the end of my long teaching career. However, given that most *early* American history textbooks suffer from the same unreadability problem as most *modern* American history textbooks, I felt compelled to put my time and effort into producing another *anti-textbook*—my first *anti-textbook* was *Making History: A Personal Approach to Modern American History*. This book is being written in the same vein to provide a personal and concise approach to surveying early American history in an exciting way that is not afraid to break from the tired mold of the textbooks produced by multi-million-dollar publishers.

Where to begin? Like a circle, the starting point may also be the ending point. Such is the thinking of most Indigenous societies today and from our ancient past. Modern society has taught us to think linearly through never-ending progress and innovation. What if we could get in touch with our ancient selves? According to anthropologists, we are all from the Great Rift Valley of East Africa, right? What if we could re-adopt the wisdom of our ancestors and mesh it with modern technology? Could that make us whole again? As for this book, *I'm An American: A Personal Approach to Early American History*, our starting point is with the first inhabitants of the continent known as North America and of the land that has come to be known as the nation of the United States, but those ancient people were not always here, they came from somewhere else, so we must go back further.

I'm An American is about identity. When I travel abroad, and someone asks me where I'm from, I usually say the United States. Then, they may ask where in the USA, and I say California. What city? Glendora. "Never heard of it," is the usual reply, or they confuse it with Glendale. So, if pressed, I say Los Angeles. But, initially, do I call myself an Angelino? A Californian? No, I say, "I'm an American." Race or ethnicity might enter the conversation. Am I a Caucasian American? A European American? A Norwegian American? No, I usually say, "I'm an American." But what does that mean? Who am I? This book will explore early American history from the Great Migration of 15,000 years ago through the American Civil War. Here are the components of this book:

Introduction: Defining America
Chapter One: Initiating America
Chapter Two: Discovering America
Chapter Three: Colonizing America
Chapter Four: Revolutionizing America
Chapter Five: Founding America
Chapter Six: Building America
Chapter Seven: Reforming America
Chapter Eight: Dividing America
Conclusion: Claiming America

Additionally, each chapter will have a personal history comic book page relating to the historical era covered. I have found that students enjoyed the comic book pages illustrated by Gary Dumm in *Making History,* so I figured they would want me to include new ones drawn by the maestro for this new book. Most history textbooks used for the early and modern US history courses are in two volumes with the same title. With this book, I have now written two stand-alone books covering the timeframe necessary for the American history survey courses required for most colleges and universities.

So, how is this book's approach different? Why is it an *anti-textbook*? It is different than the standard textbook because it is written by one person who is not afraid. I am bound to no one except myself and my students, which is a sacred commitment. I am at the end of my career and not looking for another one. My mission is to continue to inspire and empower young minds for as long as possible. We must not be timid in examining our nation's history. We must be heralds of truth and offer brilliantly inspired perspectives, not philosophical dogma, not socially acceptable dry facts, not an "accountant's truth." Keeping in mind that art is more valuable than such lifeless truth, in the words of German filmmaker Werner Herzog, this is an "ecstatic truth." Let us take a chance, take history personally, be bold, mount up, and make history. We ride at dawn!

CHAPTER ONE

Initiating America

> Objectives
> 1. Identify the earliest human civilizations.
> 2. Understand how humans came to the Americas.
> 3. Describe pre-Columbian Native American culture.
> 4. Compare and contrast Native American tribes.

In Ken Burns' sweeping documentary film *The West*, Native American anthropologist and director of the Smithsonian Institute's American Indian Program, JoAllyn Archambault, offers an honest and realistic appraisal of Native American culture before European contact.

"You know there's this marvelous stereotype out there that before white people came, the world here was perfect, that people lived in paradise in which they were the most elegant, the most moral, the most elevated of all humanity. That's not true. We were human beings, and we did things that all human beings do, and some of it was elevated and marvelous and admirable, and some it was pretty horrible." As historians, we must take a long, hard look at the past and make assessments based on evidence rather than wishful thinking and current popular narratives. I call this process thinking in time.

The Americas were home to thriving Indigenous cultures thousands of years before European contact. Each of those Native American societies adapted to their environment and created rich civilizations that would be forever changed with the arrival of the Italian explorer Christopher Columbus. The subsequent encounters between the Old and New Worlds became known as the Columbian Exchange. A worldwide exchange of knowledge, technology, culture, animals, people, plants, and disease has had both positive and negative effects and has left a lasting impact on our historical development—terrible things cannot all be blamed on Columbus. For instance, as Native American societies grew and began farming and living closer together, disease began to take its toll on Indigenous societies long before Columbus arrived. Before we delve into early Native American culture, let us travel further back in time.

As many people have done, I submitted my DNA sample to a company that traces human ancestry. I was not surprised to learn that my ancestry is primarily Scandinavian. I already knew that my relatives on both sides were all from Northern

Norway and a few from Northern Sweden, going back to the mid-1600s. However, DNA testing allowed me to see migration maps for my haplogroup. On my mom's side, my ancestors came from East Africa, through Egypt, the Middle East, and Turkey, and finally into Europe. On my father's side, we came from East Africa, Mesopotamia (Iraq), Persia (Iran), Central Eurasia, and finally into Western Europe. What impacted me the most was that we are all from the same original human ancestors, a human family. We may vary in size, shape, race, ethnicity, culture, language, and religion, but we are all human—brothers and sisters.

According to anthropologists and archeologists, modern humans evolved in the Great Rift Valley of East Africa approximately 300,000 years ago. Those humans, who were hunter-gatherers, migrated out of Africa, eventually forming major civilizations and ultimately reaching North, Central, and South America. The first human civilizations developed between 4000 and 1200 BC.

1. Mesopotamia (modern-day Iraq) from 4000–3500 BC
2. Indus Valley (modern-day India and Pakistan) from 3300 BC
3. Egypt from 3100 BC
4. China from 2000 BC
5. Peru, 1200 BC
6. Mesoamerica (modern-day Mexico) around 1200 BC

The first humans arrived in North America, possibly 16,000 years ago, during the last Ice Age, when the continent of Asia was connected to North America via the Bering Sea Land Bridge. Some recent research points to an even earlier arrival, but those theories are still not generally accepted (e.g., the trans-Pacific migration theory and the Solutrean hypothesis, which holds that humans came to North America from Europe across the Atlantic ice pack).

Many consider the pre-Columbian era (before the arrival of Christopher Columbus) to be prehistory because of the absence of written documents. Still, pre-Columbian civilizations (i.e., Aztecs, Mayas, and Incas) had some of the world's best engineers, mathematicians, and astronomers. The surviving ruins of those civilizations stand as a testament to their knowledge and skill.

Before Norwegian explorer Leif Erikson arrived in present-day Newfoundland, Canada, around the year 1000, and before Columbus arrived in 1492, over 500 distinct Native American cultures lived in the geographic area of the United States. For centuries, tribal culture tended to be similar in that most people were hunters and gatherers living in small bands. Due to climate change, the extinction of species, and the advent of agriculture, culture and geographic diversity began to develop. The Native American tribes before Columbus were incredibly diverse. The variations of culture, language, and social structure wove a rich tapestry of life in the Americas. Here is a breakdown of some of the major regions:

1. The Arctic: The Inupiat and Aleut tribes hunted game across the tundra, subsisted on seals resting on the ice floes, and hunted whales.
2. The Subarctic: The Cree, Tsattine, and Gwich'in tribes lived in pine forests and tundra in this region.
3. The Northeast and Southeast: Home to the Iroquois, Cherokee, and many others who practiced farming and had permanent villages.
4. The Plains: The Sioux, Cheyenne, and Comanche were nomads who followed the great buffalo herds and lived in tepees.
5. The Southwest: The Navajo and Hopi built cliff pueblos and other complex dwellings. They were skilled in agriculture despite the arid land.
6. The Great Basin: The tribes of this region, like the Shoshone and Paiute, adapted to a desert environment and were nomadic hunter-gatherers.
7. California: Among many other tribes, the Chumash and Miwok subsisted on fishing, hunting, and gathering nutrient-rich acorns.
8. The Pacific Northwest: With abundant forests, fish and game, and other foods, tribes like the Tlingit and Haida were known for their totem poles, long canoes, and the potlatch ceremony.
9. The Plateau: The Nez Perce and Yakama tribes were known for their underground homes and subsisted on abundant fish and game.
10. The Hawaiian Islands: The Native Hawaiians were known for their rich culture, language, and sea navigation skills.

Figure 1.1 below shows a map of tribes in the Americas.

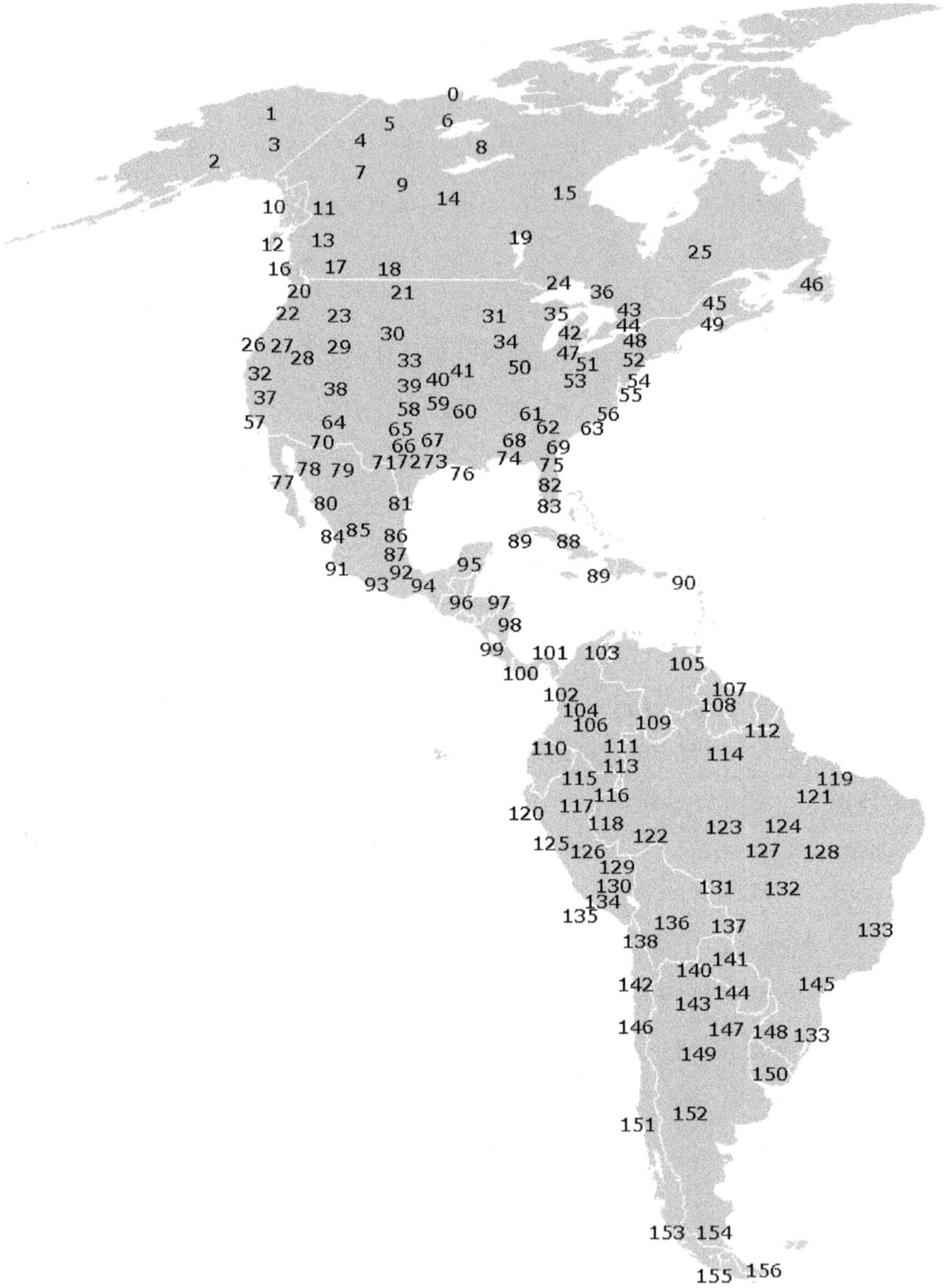
0
1
5
6
4
3
8
2
7
9
14
15
10
11
19
12
13
25
16
17
18
24
36
46
20
21
45
22
23
31
35
43
44
49
30
42
48
26
27
28
29
34
47
33
52
40
41
50
51
32
39
53
54
37
38
55
58
59
60
61
56
57
64
62
63
65
67
68
70
66
69
71
72
73
74
75
78
79
76
77
82
80
81
83
84
85
86
89
88
87
95
91
92
89
90
93
94
96
97
98
99
101
103
105
100
102
107
104
108
106
109
112
110
111
114
113
115
119
116
121
117
120
118
122
123
124
125
126
127
128
129
130
131
132
134
135
136
137
133
138
141
140
142
144
145
143
146
147
148
133
149
150
152
151
153
154
155
156

0: Inuit	39: Ute	78: Pima	118: Omagua
1: Koyukon	40: Arapaho	79: Tarahumara	119: Teremembé
2: Ingalik	41: Pawnee	80: Tepehuan	120: Tumbes Chimú
3: Tanana	42: Potawatomi	81: Coahuiltec	121: Tenetehara
4: Han	43: Algonkin	82: Timucua	122: Cawahib
5: Kutchin	44: Huron	83: Calusa	123: Mundurucú
6: Hare	45: Micmac	84: Cora	124: Timbira
7: Tutchone	46: Beothuk	85: Huichol	125: Muchic
8: Dogrib	47: Fox	86: Huaxtec	126: Shipibo
9: Kaska	48: Iroquis	87: Otomi	127: Cayapó
10: Tlingit	49: Abenaki	88: Island Arawak	128: Shavante
11: Tsimshian	50: Illini	89: Ciboney	129: Piro
12: Haida	51: Erie	90: Carib Indians (Island)	130: Campa
13: Carrier	52: Susquehannock	91: Purépecha	131: Nambicuara
14: Beaver	53: Miami	92: Totonac	132: Carajá
15: Chippewa	54: Massachusett	93: Nahuas	133: Tupinambá
16: Kwakiutl	55: Naragansett	94: Mixtec & Zapotec	134: Quechua
17: Shus-Wap	56: Delaware	95: Maya	135: Nazca
18: Sarcee	57: Chumash	96: Lenca	136: Mojo
19: Cree	58: Navajo	97: Paya	137: Bororo
20: Nootka	59: Kiowa	98: Mosquito	138: Aymará
21: Blackfoot	60: Osage	99: Nicarao	140: Sirionó
22: Chinook	61: Shawnee	100: Guaymí	141: Guato
23: Nez Perce	62: Cherokee	101: Cuna	142: Atacama
24: Ojibwa	63: Powhatan	102: Chocó	143: Mataco
25: Montagnais-Naskapi	64: Mohave	103: Guajiro	144: Caiguá
26: Yurok	65: Hopi	104: Chibcha	145: Botocudo
27: Karok	66: Pueblo	106: Guahibo	146: Diaguita
28: Modoc	67: Wichita	107: Arawak	147: Guaraní
29: Shoshone	68: Chickasaw	108: Kalinago	148: Kaingang
30: Crow	69: Catawba	109: Yanomamö	149: Abipón
31: Mandan	70: Papago	110: Paez	150: Charrúa
32: Pomo	71: Apache	111: Tucano	151: Araucanas
33: Cheyenne	72: Comanche	112: Trio	152: Puelche
34: Sioux	73: Caddo	113: Macú	153: Alacaluf
35: Menominee Sauk	74: Choctaw	114: Waiwai	154: Tehuelche
36: Ottawa	75: Creek	115: Witoto	155: Yahgan
37: Yokut	76: Natchez	116: Yagua	156: Ona
38: Paiute	77: Cochimi	117: Jivaro	

Figure 1.1: Map and List of the Indigenous People of the Americas

All Native American cultures had their own spiritual belief systems, history, art, and culture. Each tribe adapted to and impacted its environment. It should also be noted that the harsher the environment and the more difficult it was to gain resources, the fiercer and more warlike the culture was. That is why the Pacific Northwest tribes, with their abundant natural resources, were some of the most peaceful groups. Next, we will closely examine tribes that I have had experience with from a few of the regions mentioned above.

The Arctic People

The Inupiat (also known as Eskimo) people of the high north have a long and rich history dating back 4000 years. They are perfectly adapted to the harsh Arctic environment on the North Slope of Alaska, where the ice shelf is almost always fixed to the shoreline, making it difficult to reach by sea. They deeply understand their place in the environment and the proper use of natural resources. Culturally, they pride themselves on their cooperation and sharing. The traditional way of life includes hunting seals, caribou, and bowhead whales. Whale hunting is necessary for their survival and for building community and cooperation in their culture. The whale is at the center of their culture, and when the Inupiat have a successful whale hunt, they thank the whale for its life and spirit, and the food is distributed to the entire community. British explorers contacted the Inupiat on the North Slope in 1826, choosing Barrow for the town name (the northernmost settlement in North America). However, the natives called it Ukpiaġvik, "the place for hunting snowy owls." The commercial whaling ships came later in the mid-1800s and dramatically impacted life for the Inupiat (e.g., guns, alcohol, sugar, and diseases). The oil and gas industry descended upon the North Slope in the 20th century, bringing even more changes. The Inupiat still head out to the sea ice to hunt, and the Arctic provides 24 hours of sunlight in the summer and 24 hours of darkness in the fall and winter. Polar bears are a constant threat. People have lived in Barrow for 4,000 years, currently with a population of 4,400 residents. I had a unique experience in Barrow, which I will now share with you, dear reader.

My dream of college teaching came true when I started as a part-time instructor at Seattle Central Community College in the Fall of 1992, but I continued to apply for full-time work. One full-time job that I interviewed for was in Barrow, Alaska. Precisely 15 years after that short summer that I worked in South Naknek, Alaska, I arrived in the North Slope, the ice frontier. When my plane landed in Barrow, I was shocked at the condition of the place. My first impression was that Barrow was the most run-down, messy town I had ever seen. The houses were little more than glorified shacks with no paint, just worn and weathered boards. Junk was strewn everywhere, and old cars, washers, and other assorted pieces of trash were just a few items. The roads were dirt, and dust blew over everything, leaving a faint light brown coating on the town. Later, I figured out that the severe weather would strip paint off the walls of the buildings, so it was useless to spruce up your house.

Barrow is the northernmost town in North America. The Arctic ice hugged up against the beach year-round. Barrow had grown remarkably since the 1970s with the North Slope oil drilling opening at Prudhoe Bay. The townspeople were mostly Inupiat (who used to be called Eskimo). One of the teachers at the college met me at the airport. He told me a little about the town and put me in the Arctic Hotel. It looked like a hotel from an old Western movie. My window overlooked the beach and the ice. The Inupiat people I had seen since my arrival impressed me with their calmness and smiles.

It was about 11:30 p.m. when I decided to take a walk. It would be light all night, so I didn't have to worry about darkness. I walked down by the shoreline and noticed the sand's dark coarseness. I wandered the beach for a while, leaning into the gusty, freezing wind. My thoughts drifted back to my walks around the abandoned canneries at South Naknek. Then, I heard a voice from the sandy ledge above. An Inupiat man with a black baseball cap smiled down at me as he sat cross-legged on the ledge.

"Where you are standing was the old village," he said.

"Really," I said, "what happened to it?"

"The sea takes away what it gives sometimes," he said with a grin that revealed several missing teeth.

"Come up here and sit for a while," he said.

I climbed the ledge and stood next to the Inupiat man. He was about 45 years old, short, and had black horn-rimmed glasses. He told me his name was Willy.

"Are there polar bears around here?" I asked. Willy looked at me with another big grin.

"There is a big one about one hundred yards away sniffing you now. You were polar bear bait for sure on the beach," Willy said. We shared a laugh, although mine was a bit nervous.

"Here, I'll share this spot. The turf keeps you warm," he said, pointing to the grass patch where he sat. I sat down next to him cross-legged and felt warmer. I had a strange feeling that he knew that I was coming. After I told him my name, he began to tell me stories about living in Barrow. I knew that these stories had a purpose. They had no real endings or beginnings. He taught me about ice flows and whale hunting.

Figure 1.2: Me, Willy, and the Polar Bear

"The Inupiat believe you must be good people to get a whale. The whale gives himself to good people," he said. I had been against whaling, but I found his explanation of the sacred hunt satisfying.

"The whale respects good people and rewards them with his body to sustain life," he continued.

I was surprised to learn that Inupiats didn't swim. They would hunt whales in tiny sealskin boats, and if they fell out, they would drown.

"The Great Spirit would take you when he wanted to; it didn't matter whether you could swim," said Willy.

Willy was about my brother's age, so I asked if he was a Vietnam War Veteran like my brother. Willy told me that he didn't like to talk about the war.

"The Army took me from my grandfather and the ice flows and put me in a hot, steamy jungle; it was alien to me. I could only hear my grandfather's heart, and when I returned, he was gone," he said while a tear ran down his weathered brown cheek as he looked out over the ice flows.

He then began to ask me questions about what he had told me. I remembered almost everything.

"Which way is north?" Willy asked. I pointed in the wrong direction.

"You are lost," he scolded as he moved my hand so that it was pointed north. "Remember, north is where your heart leads you," he added.

I told Willy that I had to get back to the hotel room. As I stood up to go, he made a circular motion with his hand.

"All the living creatures, the water, and the land are as one," he said. I've met some remarkable people, and Willy is one of the most impressive. My guardian angel had a hand in my meeting with Willy. Not only did he save my life, but he also taught me some valuable lessons.

The next day, a middle-aged, lovely Inupiat woman met me at the Arctic Hotel, having been assigned to show me around the town. She told me about her people and the village and their challenges. She took me to a traditional blanket toss where tourists were thrown high into the air and act goofy.

"You want to try?" she asked.

"No, thank you," I said. I felt it was disrespectful to participate in one of the Inupiat rituals along with the silly, gawking tourists. She seemed to be testing me. Then, I mentioned that I'd met Willy in the regular course of our conversation about the history of her people.

"You saw Willy?" she said with a surprised look on her otherwise calm face.

"Yes, we talked for quite a while," I said. She acted like I was mistaken, shaking her head.

"Are you sure?" she asked. I described Willy to her. She paused long as we stood there, the Arctic breeze biting my face.

"That is something," she said laconically. I mentioned Willy to a few other college administration people, and they reacted similarly to my guide. It was starting to get a little weird.

I then began to think that they didn't believe me. Later, I learned that American humorist Will Rogers had died in a plane crash in Barrow in 1935. "I never met a man I didn't like" was his famous dictum. Will Rogers has always been one of my favorite Americans. Will and Willy both had something to teach me. Then, in a sudden moment of clarity, it occurred to me that people thought it strange that I met Willy because Willy wasn't among the living. I think he was a spirit, a ghost, and maybe it was surprising to the local tribal members that I'd see him because I was an outsider. But why not? I'd seen and communicated with spirits my whole life. I searched for any information about Willy online but to no avail. Ultimately, I didn't get the job in Barrow, but the experience left me feeling closer to my destination in life, although I still had a long way to go.

The Plains People

The Plains Indians lived in the grassland region known as the Great Plains, stretching from the Rocky Mountains to the Mississippi River in modern-day Canada and the United States. The tribes of this region each had their distinct language and culture. They relied on the grasslands, which provided abundant resources like buffalo and other game, as well as plenty of fresh water and wood. The Lakota are one of the three subcultures of the Sioux people. Their language likely originated from the lower Mississippi River region or Ohio Valley. Lakota legends say that they lived near the Great Lakes and were agriculturalists. Disputes with other tribes pushed them onto the Great Plains in the 17th century. By the 16th century, horses had been reintroduced to the Americas by the Spanish. The Lakota became skilled riders and transformed into a warrior and hunting culture. The following story documents my experience with a Lakota Sioux man named Phil Red Eagle.

I first met Phil Red Eagle in 1996. It was an eventful year: My daughter Caitlin was born, my father's health was declining rapidly because he was plagued by both Alzheimer's and Parkinson's, and I married my third wife, Heather. My good friend David Willson introduced me to Phil Red Eagle, a Lakota Sioux. Phil authored a unique book about the Vietnam War called *Red Earth*. It was one of the few books on the war written by a Native American. David used to arrange a Vietnam War Writers' Symposium every year, and Phil was one of the readers. I was impressed with his story and storytelling. David and I were invited to Phil Red Eagle's birthday party, and all the guests had to bring a poem or short prose piece to read, no presents. I thought it was a good idea. I got into poetry very seriously in 1995, although I had written poems since I was a teenager. There were neo-beat poetry open mic readings in Auburn and Tacoma. It was a fun, creative, and inspirational scene.

At Phil Red Eagle's birthday party, I asked him if he would do a reading from *Red Earth* for my Vietnam War history class at Green River Community College. Also, I had a more personal reason for having Phil Red Eagle come to my class; I thought it would be an opportune time to discuss these powerfully vivid recurring visions I had been having, involving my dad. Because Phil didn't have a car or couldn't drive, I'm not sure which, I had to pick him up in Tacoma, which was a 30-minute drive one way. We sat in uncomfortable silence for most of the trip to Auburn until, finally, I broke the ice.

"So, Phil, my girlfriend has scolded me for saying Indian. She says it's derogatory, and I should say Native American. What do you prefer to be called, Indian or Native American?" I asked. Phil sat in silence for a few moments, staring straight forward.

"I prefer to be called Phil," he said laconically. So much for small talk.

We arrived at the college, and I parked on the west side of campus, close to my classroom. Phil Red Eagle followed me to the classroom in silence, and when we entered the theatre-style room, he took a seat in the front. I made my usual introductory remarks and introduced Phil. There was applause, silence, and more silence. He just sat there in the front with his back to the students. After what was probably only two minutes but seemed like an hour, he spoke.

"What do you want me to do?" he asked. I was dumbfounded.

"The students have read your book, so if you could talk about your experiences in Vietnam and the writing of your book, that would be fantastic," I answered. He sat for another minute, not moving, facing forward in silence. We could hear coughing, awkward shuffling of papers, and whispering in the room.

"Whenever you're ready, Phil," I said politely, just wanting to get this thing over with at this point. He started speaking and told some interesting stories, but he faced the front the whole time and didn't look at the students. Only when the students asked questions did he turn his head slightly. Finally, thank God, it was time for class to end. There was scattered applause, a few handshakes, and then we were off.

I was determined to get a dialogue going on the 30-minute drive back to Tacoma.

"I was lucky today. I found out that a publisher has accepted my book proposal, my second book," I said proudly.

"Define good luck," Phil demanded. I looked at him oddly, thinking he was tricky or just being complicated.

"When you get something unexpectedly, or something good happens to you," I said. Phil Red Eagle looked away momentarily; then he raised his hand to scratch his forehead. In his usual carefully chosen and deliberate speech, he continued.

"In a Western sense, yes, but my people think of good luck as being able to help someone." I thought for a long moment, then I understood.

"I've been having these dreams, well, visions really, because I'm awake," I explained.

"Visions, yes," he acknowledged.

"My dad has Alzheimer's and Parkinson's. His health is deteriorating quickly," I said before he interrupted me.

"Yes, yes," he said.

"Well, I see these giant archways, like in the Southwest, yellowish-red sandstone, very powerful," I continued.

"Yes, I see them," he said.

"I'm helping him pass through the arches," I finished.

"Do you succeed in passing through?" he asked.

"I think so, yeah, but he is reluctant," I answered.

"You have been chosen to lead your father into the next world," he said.

"Yeah, I guess I'm the closest to my father of the three siblings," I said. Then he sat again in silence. Maybe he was sleeping; I wasn't sure because it was now dark. Later, he startled me by speaking loudly.

"When do I get paid?" he asked.

"What?" I asked.

"Paid for tonight, for the lecture," he elaborated.

"I never said I was paying you, Phil. I've no money to pay you. I figured I had all the students buy and read your book, and that would be okay," I explained. He seemed annoyed with my answer and silently sat until we turned onto his street. I stopped the car, and he got out and then turned around.

"There is a message, a connection to another world in those visions," he said. "You're a seeker and a person who is gifted with the ability to see visions. You have a purpose and a big responsibility," he added.

"Thank you. Maybe we could talk more about spiritual things sometime?" I asked. Phil Red Eagle looked at me with a deadpan expression.

"No," he said as he slammed the door shut. That was the last time I talked to Phil Red Eagle.

I didn't handle the grief of my mom's passing in 1990 or my dad's death in 1999 very well. I was emotionally numb. The 1990s were tough. My relationship with Heather began to deteriorate after my dad's passing, eventually leading to a divorce in 2008. I met my current wife, Ginger, in 2007. I was lucky to meet her. Ginger's patience with me as I worked through my healing process has been remarkable. In many ways, she saved me. We were married in 2012. In the Summer of 2016, Ginger and I drove to Arches National Park in Moab, Utah. Seeing those arches had been a dream of mine for nearly 20 years; I wanted to see what would happen if I saw the arches and passed through them. I had not had recurring dreams of yellowish-red sandstone arches since 1999, when my father died. Those dreams were in color and incredibly detailed. I wasn't disappointed; the arches were beautiful. I passed through several of them, sometimes climbing some treacherous rock falls to get to them. There was no immediate spiritual connection. I wondered why. Had I waited too long? Were there different arches I was supposed to visit? No, this was the place. I've had time to reflect on this, and now I know. I needed to close that chapter of my life. My father had already passed on. This trip was about me. I didn't have to feel bad any longer about making the decision not to attach a feeding tube to my father. I did the best I could and made the best decision I could make. My brother and sister didn't want to decide, so it was left to me. Or maybe I needed to go to those arches to be motivated to write about the experience and teach others. It was a staggering realization of multiple dimensions. I needed to pass through those arches, perhaps for many reasons; Ginger helped me fulfill my destiny by accompanying and supporting me. Now, I've assumed my father's role. I became a *bestefar* (grandfather in Norwegian) on November 23, 2016, when my grandson Liam was born. You see, I'm always in the process of becoming.

The Southwest People

To represent the tribes of the American Southwest, I chose the Hopi. The Moki or Moqui (also known as Hopi) people are a subgroup of the Pueblo Indians located in northeastern Arizona on the outskirts of the Painted Desert. The Hopi are said to have descended from the Anasazi, also known as the Ancestral Pueblo). Mesa Verde National Park (in the four corners region where the borders of Colorado, Arizona, New Mexico, and Utah meet) is home to the ancient cliffside dwellings of the Anasazi. The Hopi believe they ascended from kivas (underground pits now used for sacred ceremonies) into the Fourth World. The Hopi culture is based on monogamy and matrilineal descent. They are farmers who grow corn, beans, squash, melons, and other vegetables and fruits. After the Spanish arrived, they added sheep herding as well. The division of labor made men in charge of farming, herding animals, building homes, performing ceremonies, and making moccasins and other clothing. Women made baskets and pottery, watched the children, and cared for the elderly in addition to meal preparation. Hopi religious ceremonies utilize kachinas that represent gods, ancestors, and spirits.

Thomas Banyacya was born in Moenkopi, Arizona, on June 2, 1909. He lived on the Hopi reservation, resisted the draft in World War II, and was sent to prison. Prompted by the destruction of the war and the atomic bombings of Japan, he and three other Hopi were named by the elders in 1948 to bring traditional Hopi wisdom to the world and reveal prophecies. Thomas spent the next 50 years on this sacred mission, warning the world of impending doom if we did not change our ways. The Hopi religious tradition, dating back almost 1000 years (tied to the Great Spirit and Guardian of the Earth named Maasau'u), assigns them the duty of preserving Earth's natural balance and warning us how to avoid extinction. Thomas Banyacya explained that Hopi means "peaceful" and that his people reject fighting in wars. His moral stand even influenced President Dwight D. Eisenhower, who was instrumental in giving the Hopi conscientious objector status for the military draft. He was also able to forge alliances with other tribes and helped bring about a renaissance of Native American culture. He traveled the world, often with difficulty because he refused to obtain a US passport, on a Hopi passport with a buckskin cover. He even spoke to the United Nations General Assembly in 1992 after attempting to do so four times (the other elders advised him to always knock on the door four times). Thomas

Banyacya died on February 6, 1999. I will now share some personal history relating to this Hopi elder.

> Unbeknownst to me and my Norwegian cousin Børre, we both contacted a Hopi elder named Thomas Banyacya. Borre met Thomas in 1979, when he and his friend hitchhiked across the United States and reached Hopi land in Arizona. My cousin had been corresponding with Thomas and was invited to visit. Børre recalled that he was a remarkably worthy, humble, and mighty chief. He described him as Ghandi-like (referring to Mohandas K. Gandhi, who led the Indian people to independence from British rule). Thomas was incredibly joyful around children and took immense pleasure in good-naturedly tricking and fooling my cousin and his friend. Børre enjoyed his time with this great man and realized many of their sacred traditions.
>
> I read a newspaper article about Thomas Banyacya and was intrigued and inspired by his life story and mission. I attempted to contact him by letter in 1992 but was unsuccessful. I was unaware that my cousin Børre had met Thomas until I was doing historical research in Norway, and he casually mentioned his American adventure and experience with the Hopi. I find it interesting and more than a coincidence that we independently sought out this great Hopi medicine man. I can only imagine the vital lessons I would have learned from Thomas Banyacya. But there is still time, and I assume there will be more teachers in the years to come if I remain curious and listen to my heart.

The Pacific Northwest People

The tribes of the Pacific Northwest region were spread out from the coastal areas of southern Alaska to Northern California (Yakutat Bay to Cape Mendocino), an area known for abundant rainfall and natural resources. Among the cultural traditions of these tribes were the carving of totem poles and other wood carvings. Fishing, especially for salmon, was life-sustaining and figured prominently in their life and art. Gift-giving ceremonies known as potlatches allowed tribal members to display wealth, power, and generosity. The key tribes from the region include the Salish, Tlingit, Haida, Kwakiutl, and Nootka. Despite significant challenges, including land and fishing rights, the Pacific Northwest tribes have persevered and continue to uphold their traditions, language, and art.

My parents took me to the Washington State Fair in Puyallup when I was a young boy. I was excited about the rides, the strawberry scones, and the rodeo. I even saw my childhood hero, Roy Rogers, and his wife, Dale Evans. My mom wanted to name me Roy, but my dad insisted on Bruce. I have always wondered how different my life would be if my name were Roy. Who knows?

I was highly impressed with the bull riders and bucking broncos at the rodeo. It was my dream come true, having grown up watching cowboys on TV. I even got to see a Wild West show with real Indians. I also watched Western movies with John Wayne and loved to play cowboys and Indians in the woods by our home in Kenmore, Washington. I remember that none of us wanted to be the Indians; everybody wanted to be a cowboy. I figured it was because, as an Indian, you would have to go barefoot in the woods, and you could step on stickers! We were all a bunch of "tender foots."

As we were leaving the fair, something unexpected happened. One of the Native Americans from the Wild West Show stopped to talk to me. I was excited to meet him and overly enthusiastic to show him what a real "rootin' tootin' straight shootin'" cowboy I was. I put on quite a show. He was friendly and told me not to drag my feet or clomp around when I walked. Then he gave me some advice that has stuck with me all these decades later.

"Walk quietly, gently, and with purpose upon the Earth." This encounter with an actual Native American and a few others later helped me see reality. Not only did I discover the real history of the West, but I also found out that during World War II, the fairgrounds had been used as a Japanese American internment camp.

In 1970, when Native Americans were protesting over what was going to be done with Fort Lawton (an old US Army fort in Seattle), my mom took me to the protests. Developers wanted to build luxury homes, hotels, and resorts because the land was highly prized and had a beachfront on the Puget Sound. I remember she wore a headband that was not unlike the ones the Native American protesters were wearing. Up to that point, most of the Native Americans I had seen were the ones in John Wayne movies, Tonto, and winos on skid row in Seattle. My mom was tuned into the social changes that were going on in the 1960s. When Dr. Martin Luther King Jr. was assassinated, my parents grieved. My best friend from down the street told me his parents were glad King was shot. My parents also supported César Chávez and the United Farm Workers when they started the grape boycott. I was not allowed to eat grapes and was not happy about that. Now, I appreciate everything they taught me. I have taught my children tolerance and love just as my parents did.

The Plateau People

To represent the Plateau people, I chose the Yakama tribe. The Yakama people's history dates back at least 12,000 years to when they inhabited the Columbia River Plateau region. Archeological proof of their living in the area can be found in cave dwellings, petroglyphs, rock shelters, and camps. The Yakama were part of six groups that spoke the same language, Ichishkiin Sinwit. They lived in the watershed of the Lower Yakima River on the east side of the Cascade Mountains. Their daily lives involved fishing, hunting, gathering, and trading fish, baskets, dogs, and horses with other tribes. Like many Native Americans, the Yakama also faced forced relocation and conflicts with settlers. There are currently approximately 11,000 members of the tribe on a reservation encompassing 1.2 million acres by the Yakima River.

One of the most famous Yakama leaders was Chief Kamiakin. Although not as renowned as Sitting Bull, Geronimo, or even Chief Joseph, he distinguished himself as a key historical figure. He led an unsuccessful attempt to stop encroachment on his native land. Kamiakin was born circa 1800 in the small town of Starbuck in the southeastern corner of Washington State. A medicine man prophesied that Kamiakin would be the great warrior who would rise among the Yakama people to push back the White men. He went on a vision quest near Mount Rainier, where he received his guardian spirit. Kamiakin was very tall and strong and impressed the White fur traders he encountered. He was the first to irrigate the Yakima Valley and began to raise cattle on the abundant grasslands. Kamiakin became chief of the Yakama in 1840, and, in 1852, invited Catholic missionaries to enter Yakama land, thinking that his people would benefit. He was never baptized, but many of his people were, and they all lived peacefully until settler encroachment began in earnest.

Next came the railroad, something the missionaries had warned Kamiakin about. Washington State Territorial Governor Isaac Stevens pushed to eliminate Yakama claims to the land to make it easier to bring in settlers and expand the railway. In 1855, Governor Stevens, a dwarf, insisted on meeting with all the tribes to get them to sign a treaty. Kamiakin was resistant and encouraged other tribal leaders to hold firm and not sign treaties. The governor then threatened to go to war with the tribes, saying: "They would walk knee-deep in blood" if they did not sign. Kamiakin and the other leaders eventually signed the treaty on June 9, 1855, and it did not take long for the government to abrogate the treaty. The war between the government and the Yakama began on October 5, 1855, near Toppenish, Washington. Other battles were fought (i.e., the Battle of Union Gap), but ultimately, the Yakama were overwhelmed by superior force. Kamiakin was forced to flee into the Rocky Mountains as a fugitive. He eventually returned to the Washington Territory and died in 1877 on the

Colville Reservation near Rock Lake in the northeastern territory. Sadly, he was not allowed to rest in peace because grave robbers desecrated his burial site and stole his head, which was never recovered. A high school in Kennewick, an elementary school in Sunnyside, and a junior high school in Kirkland are all named after Chief Kamiakin.

Dear reader, I would like to share a personal story about an adventure near the Yakama Reservation on Mount Adams in Washington State. The eastern portion of Mount Adams, one of several dormant volcanoes in the Pacific Northwest, lies within reservation territory.

> I met Susanne in graduate school during my separation and divorce from my first wife, Anna. We quickly moved in together and decided to move to Seattle in the Fall of 1992 so I could find work as a teacher. I had already finished my doctoral studies and successfully defended my dissertation, so it was only a matter of waiting to graduate in the Spring of 1993 officially. My two older boys, Bjørn and Byron, stayed behind with their mother in Bowling Green, Ohio. Leaving them behind was one of the hardest things I had ever done in my life, but there were no jobs in Bowling Green, and I had lost custody of my boys in the divorce. Susanne and I lived with my father in Kenmore, Washington, and eventually found an apartment in Redmond, right next to the Microsoft campus. I taught part-time at Seattle Central Community College, and Susanne cleaned houses.
>
> In June 1993, we went camping in the mountains. I decided that Olallie Lake campground near Mount Adams would be a wonderful place to camp and hike. We set up camp, and the next day, we hiked up to the snow line on Mount Adams and sunned ourselves on the rocks. It was a glorious day. We could see Mount Rainier, Mount Saint Helens, Mount Baker, and Glacier Peak in the distance. We decided to go cross-country and not follow the main trail on the way down.
>
> We eventually followed a small animal trail, and it was on the edge of that trail that I found an odd object. It looked only like a twisted root at first, but upon further inspection, I saw that it looked ancient and had evidence of human shaping. Half covered by debris, I assumed it had been there for ages. The closer I looked at the object, the stranger it appeared. It was a human figure, a male figure.
>
> "What do you think it is?" I asked.
>
> "I don't know. Maybe you should leave it here," said Susanne. I shook my head no, put the object in my pack, and headed to the camp. We made a fire, cooked dinner, and then sat around the fire relaxing. I had the object in my hand and examined it as the evening passed. Finally, it was time for bed.

Figure 1.3: Treetop Warriors

Later that night, I fell into an uneasy sleep. At about midnight, I woke up because I heard some strange noises, like people chanting. I woke Susanne up and asked her if she had heard anything, but she had not. The chanting sounds grew louder than before, and I got a weird tingling sensation and a hyper-awareness. Maybe the earthly and spirit worlds were colliding, I thought. I put my pants back on, unzipped the tent flap, and sat on my sleeping bag, staring out into the starry night, holding the strange object that had been in my pants pocket when we went to sleep. I started speaking in a peculiar way that freaked out Susanne.

"The ancient people, the grandfathers and grandmothers, awaken at night," I said.

"Stop it, you're scaring me," said Susanne.

"The ghost moon calls," I said as I pointed to the starry sky and the full moon with an unusual aura. I looked at Susanne and held her hand to reassure her.

"I'm not sure what's going on," I told her, "I think I hear the voices of ancient Indians."

"You mean Native Americans," she said, correcting me.

"Sure, whatever," I said.

"I see several Indians moving around a campfire," I said.

"I don't see any Indians, ah, Native Americans," she said, correcting herself mid-sentence. The trees stood and witnessed as the ancient people began their dance. I could hear a distant drum.

"Do you hear it?" I asked.

"Do I hear what?" she asked.

"A heartbeat and a drum," I said. Susanne looked at me like I was crazy, but the vision continued. The fire shadows grew tall in the trees as the ancient Indians danced around the campfire. I could make out the words that they sang, and I repeated them.

"Ohh wahh tay, ohh wahh tay, kom sa yeay, kom sa yeay," I sang as I joined in. "Look," I said, "they're rising to fill their fire-shadow."

"You're kidding, right?" Susanne asked. The ancient warriors then flew to the treetops. I could see them move off toward the mountain. A procession of treetop warriors. I explained this to Susanne, but she said she didn't see or hear anything and was tired.

After a few minutes, I heard another voice, a man speaking in English.

"My name is Leon; I'm a medicine man," he said. I looked around but didn't see him; I only heard his voice.

"We're having the same vision," he said.

"What's going on?" I asked.

"The ancient ones follow the treetop aerial pathways," he said.

"Where are you?" I asked. Nothing, just silence. I didn't hear any more. Then, off in the distance toward the mountain, the Indians call Pahto or Klickitat, gliding through the night, the starry night, the ghost moon night, the treetop warriors faded away.

When we returned home, I called the Yakama tribe. Their reservation was very near the spot where we were camping. A lady from the Yakama Cultural Center answered, and I told her about the object I had found and my vision.

"We don't know anyone named Leon," she said tersely.

"He's a medicine man," I said. There was a long pause.

"No," she said.

"Are you sure that..." I was beginning to ask when she interrupted.

"Where's the artifact?" she asked.

"I have it right here in my hand," I answered.

"People often take sacred objects from our land," she said.

"I'm sorry...I didn't mean..." I said.

"Put it back," she insisted.

"You don't want to study it?" I asked. She didn't answer, and then she hung up the phone. Susanne looked at me sympathetically.

"You should put it back, even though I don't believe in all of that stuff," said Susanne.

"I don't have the luxury of believing or not believing. These things happen to me whether I want them to or not," I added.

By the way, Kenneth Arnold, the civilian pilot who first spotted UFOs in 1947 and whose sighting later started the term "flying saucers," spotted the string of his UFOs traveling from Mount Rainier to Mount Adams.

I kept the object but fully intended to go back to Mount Adams to return it. I had a series of hard luck incidents in the next three years. Susanne and I were fighting and arguing; we were having money problems and wandered from place to place, unable to settle down, even though we were in a committed relationship. I didn't want her to leave and go back to Austria.

Ultimately, I started a relationship with the woman who would become my next wife, Heather. That was the end of my rocky relationship with Susanne. I take the blame. Susanne returned to Austria. Heather and I got married soon after. We also had a baby right away, my daughter Caitlin. By then, we lived in Auburn, and I taught at Green River Community College. Although I was hoping for the best, it wasn't long until my relationship with Heather began to deteriorate; my fault, and I was miserable again.

One day, I saw the object I had found on Mount Adams as we were packing to move again. I thought about everything that had happened since I found it. Nothing had gone well. Out of frustration, I threw the object into the attic space above the attached garage in our rental house. I assume it's still there today, unbeknownst to the homeowners or renters.

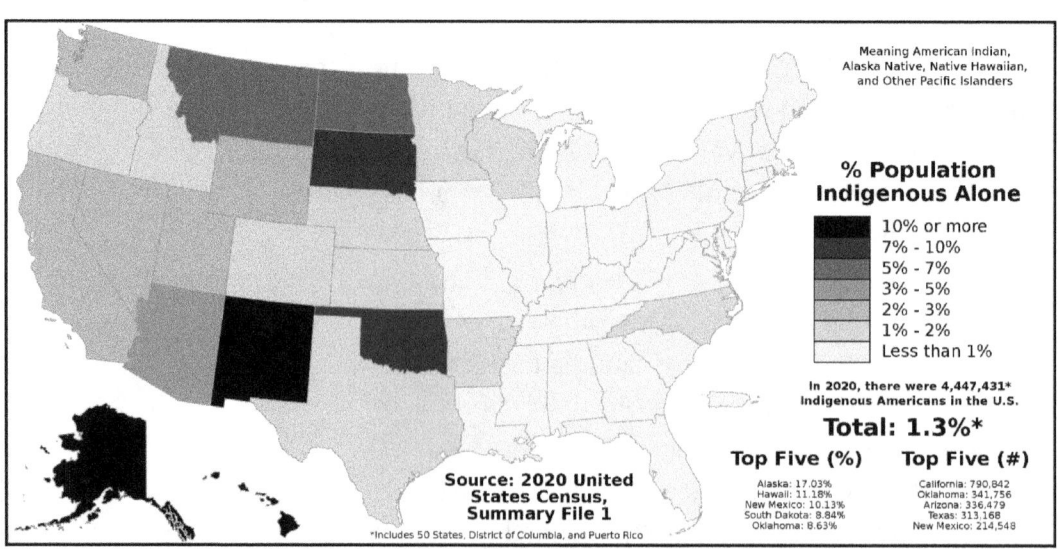

Figure 1.4: Percentage of Native Americans Living in Each State in 2020

Above is a map of the United States showing the percentage of Native Americans living in each state. It is hard to imagine American history without Native Americans, but these tribes are not just a thing of the past. They are alive, and tribal members are persevering and preserving their heritage, which is so vital to us all.

Conclusion

Although there are certain common elements, Native American cultures vary greatly. When the Europeans made contact, first Leif Erikson and nearly five hundred years later, Columbus, the Native Americans spoke hundreds of different languages, lived in small groups or large cities, were settled or were nomadic, and were friendly and welcoming or suspicious, and warlike, and everything in between. They were real people with real problems, like everybody else. What is clear is that the meeting of Old and New Worlds would change everything for everybody.

Recommended Sources

"Bering Land Bridge formed surprisingly late during last ice age." https://new.nsf.gov/news/bering-land-bridge-formed-surprisingly-late-during

"Evidence of humans in North America during the Last Glacial Maximum." https://www.science.org/doi/10.1126/science.abg7586

Tom D. Dillehay, *The Settlement of the Americas: A New Prehistory* (New York: Basic Books, 2000).

Credits

Figure 1.1: Map of the Indigenous People of the Americas. https://upload.wikimedia.org/wikipedia/commons/2/28/Indigenous_peoples_americas_1535.png and https://commons.wikimedia.org/wiki/File:Indigenous_peoples_americas_1535.png

Figure 1.2: Me, Willy, and the Polar Bear. Illustration by Gary Dumm in *Timeless: A Paranormal Personal History* by Bruce Olav Solheim.

Figure 1.3: Treetop Warriors. Illustration by Gary Dumm in *Timeless: A Paranormal Personal History* by Bruce Olav Solheim.

Figure 1.4: Percentage of Native Americans Living in Each State in 2020. https://upload.wikimedia.org/wikipedia/commons/thumb/f/f2/Indigenous_Americans_by_state.svg/2560px-Indigenous_Americans_by_state.svg.png

CHAPTER TWO

Discovering America

> Objectives
> 1. Understand the significance of the Columbian Exchange.
> 2. Compare and contrast the voyages of Leif Erikson and Christopher Columbus.
> 3. Uncover the motivations for European exploration of the Americas.
> 4. Compare the Spanish, English, and French colonial experience and impact.

Over five hundred years before Columbus, Leif Erikson sailed off-course en route to Greenland and reached North America. His father, Erik the Red, founded the first European settlement in Greenland. Leif called his discovery Vinland. Of course, Native Americans had already been in North America, so it was not a discovery as much as a lucky accident that he became the first European to set foot in the Americas. Archeological evidence corroborates ancient Viking sagas that point to L'Anse aux Meadows in northern Newfoundland, Canada, as Leif Erikson's landing spot. After he returned to Greenland, his brother Thorvald led another expedition to Vinland but could not establish a settlement due to skirmishes with Native Americans in the area. Upon Congressional approval in 1964, President Lyndon B. Johnson declared October 9 as Leif Erikson Day.

Figure 2.1: Leif Erikson Discovers America

Dear reader, I would like to share a personal story related to this topic of exploration. All of us must explore our roots and ancestry to discover who we are. This is such a story.

> In 1992, I traveled to Norway to conduct research for my doctoral dissertation. I visited the Defense Department Archives, the National Archives, and the Labor Party Archives. I chose to write my dissertation on Nordic foreign policy during the Cold War and how the five Nordic countries balanced their security interests in relation to pressure from the two superpowers. I compared this Nordic Balance to a human hand. Each finger (like each Nordic country) can move independently of the others, adjusting its movement forward and backward, up and down. Each of the five fingers is attached to the palm, which simultaneously allows for this articulation and provides the security of a base.
>
> I was so focused and busy with my research that I didn't thoroughly appreciate being in Norway and exploring my roots. After completing my research, I flew to northern Norway, where my father lived. Since my mother died in 1990, Dad would stay in Norway for the spring and summer and then return to Seattle for the rest of the year. Norway is a land of mountains and oceans. The land meets the sea through deep fjords that carve far inland. It's also a land of small farms and towns. The pace of life up north is slow. People have time to live and to know one another. When I arrived up north and was away from the urban Oslo environment and the pressure of my research, I had time to consider my heritage. I thought about how my roots stretched across the seas thousands of miles and years ago. Since I was a little boy, I've dreamed of returning to live in Norway. Mom and Dad had made a life for us in the New World. I'm of the New World, but because I grew up with the Norwegian language, customs, and traditions, I'm part of the Old as well.
>
> When I arrived in Andøya Island, two hundred miles above the Arctic Circle, my dad said we should walk up to the graveyard at the base of the mountains. We started by hiking straight up from the back of our property. The island's mountainous spine rises above the peat bogs and little birch trees in the lower elevations. As we worked our way through the birch forest, we saw the road that led to the village cemetery. We spent about 15 minutes at the graveyard visiting the graves of my eldest brother Bjørn, my grandparents, and my mother. Dad had purchased a double headstone, so there was room for his name when the time came. I couldn't think of a more peaceful and beautiful place to be buried—nestled amongst the birch trees, under the mountains, and overlooking the fjord.
>
> "Let's go," Dad said as he hurried out of the graveyard and headed further south on the dirt road. It was all I could do to keep up with this 77-year-old man. We

crossed the Åse River, named after the village, and then came to a clearing with a gently sloped mound.

"Oh, this is where we have the midsummer bonfire," I said.

"Ya, and it's also where our ancestors are buried," said Dad. I looked at him with curiosity.

"We were just at the graveyard," I said.

"Before there were Christians, people were buried here, on Dungen; they were Viking people," Dad said with pride.

"Dungen?" I asked.

"Ya, that is what we call this place," he said in Norwegian.

"So, these are my Viking ancestors?" I asked.

"Ya," he answered. I walked to the top of the mound, and suddenly I was overwhelmed. I felt the sea breeze from the fjord and heard the ageless whispers of my ancestors, and I was at home. For the first time, I realized what this unique island meant to me. It wasn't just the island where my parents, my eldest brother, and my sister were born; it was my spiritual inheritance and my destiny. I felt a sacred connection as I stood on the burial mound of my forbearers from 1000 years ago. My dad knew our walk's importance because he had planned this, but he wasn't done.

"Let's go," he said as he took off quickly. We continued south until the dirt road hugged close to the steep mountainside.

"There it is," he said as he pointed to a group of stones on the slope.

"That is the spot where your mom and I made coffee and ate lunch on warm summer days during haying season," he remarked sadly. They would cut the grass and dry it on wire fences by hand. After the grass had dried and turned to hay, they would collect it and store it in their barns to feed their animals for the winter. Dad walked up to the pile of stones and knelt.

"We used these to surround the fire," he said.

"Are you sure it's the same spot?" I asked. Dad ignored my question as he dug beneath the stones, a man in his twilight years unearthing his cherished memories. He dug through the grass and a half-century's worth of dark, fertile soil as I stood and watched. From the hole he had just dug, he produced some charred sticks.

"These were from our campfires," he said.

"Wow, that's amazing," I said. Then, Dad pulled out a piece of broken, off-white porcelain from the hole. It was a handle attached to half of a coffee cup. He gathered a few more pieces and laid them out on the stones in the sun.

"This was one of the cups your mother and I used," he said, overcome with emotion, a tear running down his cheek.

"I remember your mom accidentally dropped the cup and broke it," he said with a smile. We stood and stared at the broken coffee cup, its white ceramic stained by the soil. I imagined the cutting of the hay on those steep sunny slopes so long ago. I saw their small fire and the boiling water. I saw my father as a young man, teasing my mother, as he often did later in life. I could hear my mother's voice, speaking in their unique dialect, as I pictured them in their youth. Then, my father put the coffee cup back into the hole and carefully covered it.

"Shouldn't we take it home and keep it?" I asked.

"No, it's best to leave it here. It belongs here," Dad remarked solemnly. My father had finished teaching me.

It wasn't unusual for me to use a hand to symbolize my doctoral dissertation. Hands are remarkable, and everyone's hands tell a story. One of the things I remember most about Dad was his hands. He had powerful hands. Decades of hard labor in fishing and construction had made them that way. They were hands that rubbed my forehead when I was a little boy with a fever, and they were the hands that spanked me when I misbehaved. They were the hands that provided for us as a family. I watched his hands as he re-buried the broken coffee cup. Although they were still strong, they had begun to shake sometimes, revealing his advanced age. I learned of rock and soil, flesh and blood, distant memories, and sacred moments that day. We stood looking out over the fjord for a while as the wind blew and time ticked away slowly and steadily.

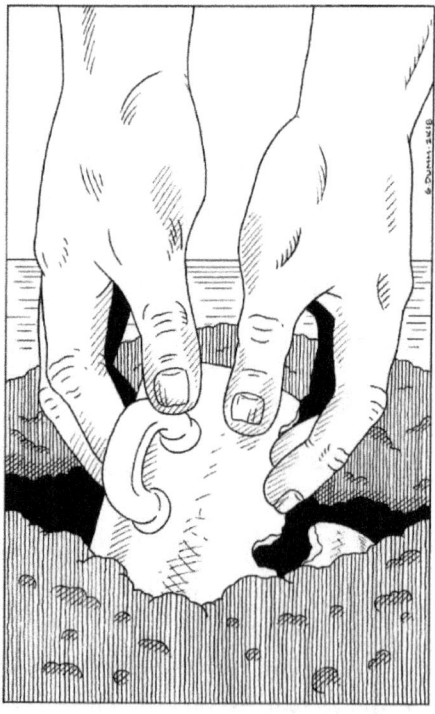

Figure 2.2: The Coffee Cup

Many traditional histories began with the story of Christopher Columbus discovering America. Not only was Columbus not the first person to set foot in the Americas (he reached the West Indies in the Caribbean), but he was also not even the first European to reach the New World. Nonetheless, Columbus's impact on the Americas is without question as it blazed the trail for further exploration and, eventually, colonization. Spain, Portugal, France, the Netherlands, and England saw the Americas as a source of precious metals, exotic goods, trade, land, slaves, and religious converts. Native Americans initially saw the Europeans as economic and military partners, but as European desire for land increased, so did tensions between the people of the Old and New Worlds. We will now look at how Spain, France, the Netherlands, Portugal, and England each established colonies in the New World.

Figure 2.3: Columbus Taking Possession

Spain

Columbus represented Spain even though he was Italian, so the Spanish first established permanent American colonies. Although the effects of European wars and slave raids on Native American societies were devastating, disease epidemics were perhaps the most crucial factor in allowing European conquest of the Americas. As the doors were thrown open to the continent, conquistadors like Hernán Cortés and Francisco Pizarro arrived and were able to conquer the well-established and mighty Aztec and Inca empires (1521 and 1535 respectively). Collectively known as New Spain, the Spanish colonies encompassed the Southwestern part of the modern-day United States, Mexico, the Caribbean, and Central and South America. New Spain was just part of Spain's global empire. They introduced Catholicism and European-style government and farming methods. In the process, the Native Americans were exploited, their ranks decimated, and the African slave trade became a fixture in the Spanish colonial economy. La Isabela, on the island of Hispaniola (modern-day Haiti and Dominican Republic), was the first Spanish colony established by Columbus. St. Augustine, Florida, established by Pedro Menéndez de Avilés (a Spanish soldier) in 1565, is the oldest European settlement in the United States. The Spanish conquistadors entered the Americas bent on conquest and exploration. Let us take a closer look.

Hernán Cortés led the conquest of the Aztec Empire between 1519 and 1521. His expeditions brought Spanish rule to Central America and parts of what is now the southern and western United States. Francisco Pizarro led the conquest of the Inca Empire in Peru in 1533. The conquistadors were after gold and spoiled for a fight. Eventually, they were replaced by government officials from Spain who could solidify control over territories stretching from South America to parts of what is now the United States. We will now go into more depth in understanding the story of one of these Spanish explorers.

Álvar Núñez Cabeza de Vaca was a Spanish explorer who served as a treasurer on an expedition to the New World led by Pánfilo de Narváez in 1528. The expedition reached Tampa Bay, Florida, but most of the personnel had died. By the time they reached Galveston, Texas, only 15 survived. Eventually, Cabeza de Vaca and three others were the only remaining explorers left, as they then spent eight years living with nomadic Native American tribes. Cabeza de Vaca became a trader and a healer and had some remarkable experiences living with the Native Americans.

Cabeza de Vaca and his companions ensured their survival by becoming slaves and thereby learned of the various customs, everyday lives, and languages of the tribes they encountered. He wrote about his experiences in a journal he kept. He noted that the Indigenous people were not "animal-like savages" as the conquistadors had described them. Cabeza de Vaca and his friends were attacked on occasion but explained that it was a natural reaction by the Native Americans to attack strangers on their land. He also wrote about their kindness and selflessness and described how one tribe fed and sheltered them when they were near death. Notably, he also observed that each tribe was unique and could not be defined through blanket characterizations. Cabeza de Vaca tried to bring peace and spread the word of Jesus Christ in his travels, often facing threats from fellow Spanish explorers. His insightful accounts provided honest impressions of the Native Americans and their displays of compassion and cultural reciprocity, emphasizing the complexity and diversity of American Indigenous societies. In 1536, he returned to Mexico and eventually explored Brazil and Paraguay.

Figure 2.4: Portrait of Álvar Núñez Cabeza de Vaca

Spain pushed further into North America. Hernando de Soto explored the southeastern United States from 1539 to 1542, hoping to find gold, but instead, he left behind a trail of death from European diseases unknown to Native Americans. Francisco Vásquez de Coronado entered Mexico, then called New Spain, in 1535. He also pursued gold and explored the southwestern United States. He fought with Native Americans in New Mexico from 1540 to 1542. He did not discover gold and silver and was bankrupt from the expedition.

The Netherlands

The Dutch Republic (Holland) was formed in 1581 but formally gained independence from Spain in 1648. The Dutch colonization efforts were driven by powerful corporations like the Dutch East India Company, which began trading in Asia in 1602, and the Dutch West India Company, which began trading in 1621 in the Americas. The English Sea captain Henry Hudson worked for the Dutch East India Company as he explored New York Harbor and the Hudson River, which bears his name. Captain Hudson was initially seeking a northwest passage to Asia but soon found that trading in furs, especially beaver pelts, was quite lucrative. So, he claimed the region for the Netherlands. The Dutch named the colony New Netherlands and set up a fur trading post under the auspices of the influential Dutch West India Company. Trade with the local Algonquian and Iroquois tribes established a commercial network in the Hudson River Valley and beyond, eventually reaching the Caribbean, positioning Holland as a commercial rival to Spain in the Americas. Although other Europeans played critical roles in colonizing North America, Great Britain would have the most profound influence on the early history of the United States.

England

Like other Europeans, the English hoped to find gold and silver in North America, but they were unsuccessful, something that, at least at first, limited British colonization. The Roanoke Colony in what is now North Carolina came first but disappeared mysteriously. Often called the Lost Colony, Sir Walter Raleigh established the Roanoke Colony in 1585. By 1587, the first location was abandoned, and the colonists struggled with their environment and Native Americans. After returning to England to secure supplies for the struggling colony, Governor John White returned to Roanoke in 1590 to find it deserted, with no trace of the 115 colonists. The only clue was a mysterious inscription (still unsolved) on a wood post: "Croatoan." The English were more successful in establishing another colony, this time at Jamestown (1607) in present-day Virginia.

In 1607, The Virginia Company sent one hundred colonists to an area on the James River in Virginia to establish a British colony in the name of King James I. The settlers had a high mortality rate caused by disease, famine, and conflict with the native inhabitants. A marriage between Englishman John Rolfe and Pocahontas, the daughter of a local Native American chief from the Powhatan tribe, helped establish the colony, as did successful tobacco cultivation. Jamestown expanded east and served as the foundation for future English settlements in America.

Figure 2.5: The Landing of the Pilgrims at Plymouth Rock

The much-ballyhooed Pilgrims established a second British colony in modern-day Massachusetts in 1620. They were Puritan separatists from the Church of England who were escaping persecution at home and searching for religious freedom. The Pilgrims were initially supposed to land near the mouth of the Hudson River (now New York City), but storms blew them off course, and they ended up near Cape Cod in Plymouth (now Massachusetts). They collectively signed the Mayflower Compact to lay out the governance of their new colony. The Pilgrims, under the leadership of William Bradford, were able to negotiate with the Wampanoag Confederation, who showed them how to plant corn, beans, and squash. The ceremony became known as Thanksgiving, when they all came together for a big feast. Although Plymouth was North America's second permanent English colony, it never had as many settlers as the other colonies. Eventually, Plymouth combined with the much larger Massachusetts Bay colony in 1691, and thereby, as Puritans, left their mark on our nation. We will now see how other European countries contributed to the colonization of America, starting with France.

France

The French colonization of the Americas significantly shaped and influenced the region's economies, cultures, languages, and history. France came to the New World attempting to find a quicker route to the Pacific Ocean in pursuit of wealth through trade. French King Francis I sent Italian explorer Giovanni da Verrazzano to the East coast of North America, from Newfoundland to Florida, in 1524. Verrazzano explored New York Harbor and heightened French interest in the Americas. In 1534, French explorer Jacques Cartier took the first of his three voyages to the New World, where he carefully navigated and charted the coast of Newfoundland and the St. Lawrence River. He officially declared the area New France when he planted a cross at the Gaspé Peninsula. The Gulf of St. Lawrence and the St. Lawrence River became essential trade routes, providing access to the Great Lakes region's interior. In 1608, Samuel de Champlain founded the colony of New France and the city of Quebec. He also mapped and explored the Caribbean and the coastal areas of North America. French fur trading extended to cities such as Detroit, Green Bay, St. Louis, and New Orleans at the mouth of the Mississippi. The French colonial empire in the Americas grew to 3.9 million square miles by 1710, second only to the Spanish Empire. France left its imprint on the future United States through trade, language, architecture, cuisine, and legal systems.

Portugal

The Portuguese focused mainly on Africa, Asia, and Brazil for their colonial efforts, but they did influence North America in some crucial ways. After Columbus, an Italian named Amerigo Vespucci explored the Americas on behalf of Portugal between 1499 and 1502. Vespucci realized that the Americas were not part of Asia, and his reports inspired other Europeans to contact the New World. A German cartographer named Martin Waldseemüller was the first to label the New World. In 1507, thank goodness he named it America on his map, and not Vespucci.

Gonçalo Coelho and Estêvão Gomes explored North America's east coast in the early 16th century, but Portugal did not establish any permanent colonies. The Portuguese did impact global history through their expert navigation and by fully developing trade routes to India and Asia, which helped grow European economies. However, their role in the transatlantic slave trade had the most significant impact on North America. Portugal established Brazil as a center for sugar production and the importation of African slaves, many of whom were eventually sent to the European colonies in North America.

The Columbian Exchange

The hunger for colonies in the Americas was created by competition, as no one wanted to be left out of the land grab and the promised treasures. However, the reality was that the experience was more negative than positive both for the Europeans and the Native Americans. There was violent conflict, disease, and exploitation. All this drove the European powers to instigate the transatlantic slave trade to provide the labor necessary to meet production demand. The transportation of people, animals, plants, and diseases became known as the Columbian Exchange. Cattle, horses, pigs, wheat, rye, and smallpox came from Europe. Corn, potatoes, tobacco, beans, squash, peppers, cocoa, and syphilis came from the Americas. Sugar, rice, malaria, and yellow fever came from Africa. Sugar was king, holding as much economic importance as petroleum does today. Sugar cane plantations sprung up everywhere in the New World, especially in the Caribbean. Eventually, they mixed sugar with cocoa, creating chocolate, which Europeans could not get enough of (I cannot lie, I love chocolate too). Tobacco was also a valuable commodity coming from the Americas, and Europeans took up the habit of smoking for pleasure as opposed to the Native American use of tobacco for ceremonies. Perhaps most tragic of all was the introduction of Old World diseases to the New World, where Native Americans had no natural immunity, leading to a tremendous loss of life.

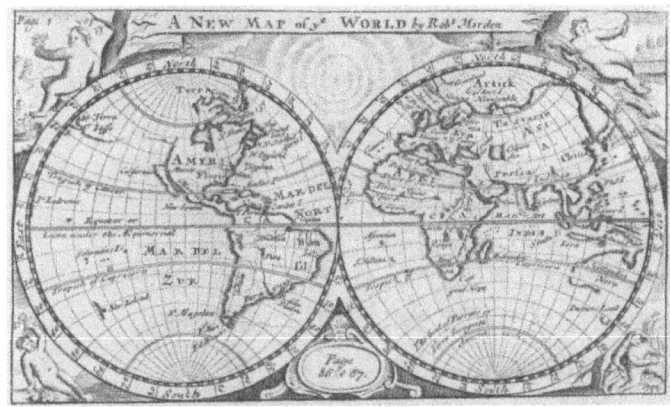

Figure 2.6: The New World and Old World

Conclusion

All the European colonial powers played a part in globalization and connecting the world through trade and exploration. Since the Crusades throughout the 11th and 12th centuries, Europeans had grown to desire goods from the East, such as exotic spices, sugar, porcelain, and silk. They obtained fur and timber from Slavic countries (where the word slave came from). However, the overland route along the Silk Road from China to the Mediterranean Sea became too treacherous and expensive. Hence, it caused Europeans to want to explore alternate trade routes by sea. They reached the Americas by accident in pursuing this sea route to China and discovered what they thought was the East Indies (therefore, they called the Native people Indians). The Europeans would come to dominate the Americas and introduce large-scale human slavery to support production and trade. Spain grew rich, as did other

Europeans, from their colonization of the Americas, but at the expense of the Native Americans and enslaved Africans.

Historians have argued over how many Native Americans perished after European contact. Some say 100 million, while others estimate only two million deaths. At the worst, perhaps 95% of Native Americans died because of European colonization. Europe's Black Death peaked at about 35% in comparison. Pandemics of smallpox, typhus, bubonic plague, influenza, mumps, and measles devastated the New World. On a more positive note, the Columbian Exchange improved nutrition for everyone in the New and Old Worlds. America's crops spawned a population explosion in Europe. The introduction of cattle and pigs gave Native Americans more sources of protein. Horses introduced by the Spaniards were quickly utilized by native tribes, especially on the Great Plains. The bridging of the Old and New Worlds separated by 10,000 years after the Bering Sea Land Bridge's closing transformed the world. Dear reader, I hope you enjoy reading about my firsthand experiences related to the topics in this book. I know that I enjoy telling my tales. In the next chapter, we will deal with perhaps the darkest story from early American history: slavery.

Recommended Sources

"Exploration of North America." https://www.history.com/topics/exploration/exploration-of-north-america.

"Leif Erikson." https://www.biography.com/history-culture/leif-eriksson.

Samuel Eliot Morison. *Admiral of the Ocean Sea*.

Credits

Figure 2.1: Leif Erikson Discovers America. Source: https://commons.wikimedia.org/wiki/File:Leif_Erikson_Discovers_America_Hans_Dahl.jpg.

Figure 2.2: The Coffee Cup. Illustration by Gary Dumm in *Timeless: A Paranormal Personal History* by Bruce Olav Solheim.

Figure 2.3: Columbus Taking Possession. Source: https://commons.wikimedia.org/wiki/File:Columbus_Taking_PossessionFXD.jpg.

Figure 2.4: Portrait of Álvar Núñez Cabeza de Vaca. Source: https://commons.wikimedia.org/wiki/File:Cabeza_de_Vaca_Portrait.jpg.

Figure 2.5: The Landing of the Pilgrims at Plymouth Rock. Source: Library of Congress. https://www.loc.gov/resource/cph.3a25752/.

Figure 2.6: The New World and Old World. Source: Lionel Pincus and Princess Firyal Map Division, The New York Public Library. (1708). https://digitalcollections.nypl.org/items/510d47df-fb48-a3d9-e040-e00a18064a99.

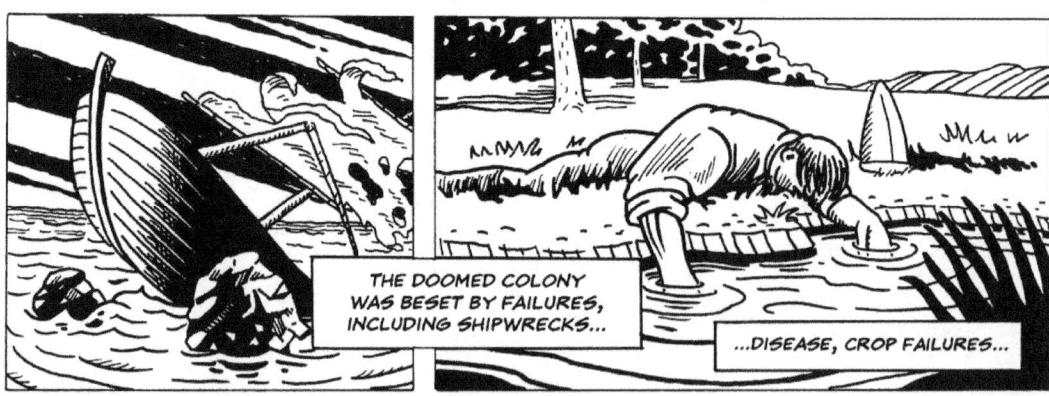

CHAPTER THREE

Colonizing America

Objectives
1. Understand the significance and legacy of slavery in America.
2. Compare and contrast the original 13 colonies.
3. Comprehend the difficulties faced by both settlers and Native Americans.
4. Uncover how the European colonists began to become Americans.

When the first colonists approached the shores of the eastern coast of North America, they could already smell the pine forests from 200 nautical miles out at sea. Such was the power of the land of the New World, beckoning them to start anew, build, and grow, but they would not be alone. The colonial period of the history of the United States spans from the early 16th century until the uniting of the Thirteen Colonies into the United States after the Revolutionary War. As we have seen in the previous chapter, the European powers, including England, France, Spain, and others, explored and established their colonies in North America.

The first permanent English colony was in Jamestown, Virginia, in 1607. The Thirteen Original Colonies (Virginia, Massachusetts, New York, Pennsylvania, Maryland, Rhode Island, Connecticut, New Hampshire, Delaware, North Carolina, South Carolina, New Jersey, and Georgia) were established on the Atlantic coast. Later, the fledgling nation began to expand westward. Each colony was unique and varied in economy, agriculture, governance, slavery, and religion. All colonies faced obstacles and challenges presented by the environment, disease, and conflicts with Native Americans. The Europeans did not want to relinquish their colonial territory, and disputes involving the major powers erupted, dragging the colonists into the battle (i.e., the French and Indian War from 1754 to 1763). The longer the colonists remained in America, the more they changed and separated themselves from England. Tensions emerged over taxation that eventually flared up into the American Revolutionary War (1775 to 1781), where the ragtag loose assembly of colonies won their independence from Great Britain, the most powerful country in the world. The colonial era laid the legal, cultural, political, and economic groundwork for the nation that emerged—the United States of America.

Let us begin by closely examining the foundation of Jamestown, the first English colony, in 1607. Then, we will describe the founding of the other colonies, providing a general description of the three major colonial regions: Southern, Middle, and New England.

Jamestown

The Jamestown Colony in Virginia was not only the first permanent English colony in North America but also the most significant in terms of its historical impact on further settlement and the eventual founding of the United States. Jamestown was founded by the Virginia Company and provided a foothold for further English colonization. The colonists suffered conflicts with Native Americans, famine, and disease. Tobacco cultivation saved the colony and led to later economic growth for Virginia. For better or worse, Jamestown also set the precedent for relations with the native inhabitants. The House of Burgesses was established in 1619, laying the groundwork for representative government in the future United States. Also, in 1619, unfortunately, as most history textbooks point out, Jamestown is known as the place where slavery began in the English colonies. Contrary to many historical texts, the first arrival of African slaves to the future United States was in 1526, not 1619.

Lucas Vázquez de Ayllón founded the Spanish colony of San Miguel de Gualdape in 1526. It was located between South Carolina and Georgia and was the first European settlement in what would become the United States. The colony only lasted for two months before the settlers were struck by disease and overcome by starvation, a hostile Native American tribe, and a slave uprising. Only 150 of the original 600 survived.

Although slavery was transatlantic, it had unique characteristics in the British colonies in North America. Virginia imported its first African slaves in 1619 as the need for labor increased for larger estates. Laws about the inheritance of landed estates were strict, so wealth and property were not broadly distributed. Tobacco planters dominated the economic, political, and social aspects of society. By 1750, nearly 40% of Virginia's population were enslaved Africans who worked long hours under the supervision of White overseers who employed physical violence to force labor. The first comprehensive slave code was passed in 1705 by the Virginia House of Burgesses. These laws ensured that children born of slaves would also be slaves, and conversion to Christianity would not save them from slavery. The code also allowed for the murder of enslaved persons and inflicted harsh punishments on slaves who struck any White person.

The year 1619, when twenty African slaves arrived in Jamestown, is not the best place to begin to tell the story of the enslavement of Africans in America. That event, as it has been presented repeatedly in historical studies and even through a government-sponsored 1619 Project, does not tell the whole story. By 1619, nearly a half million African people had been brought to the New World against their will.

The competing European powers together facilitated transatlantic slavery since the early 1500s. This includes Portugal, Spain, Great Britain, France, and the Netherlands. The Europeans can best be categorized as invaders and colonizers rather than settlers or immigrants. Even the term *illegal alien* is more applicable. The Native Americans sometimes welcomed and sometimes fought them, but none realized what would come in the New World. Africans, whether enslaved or not, provided expertise in crop cultivation and knowledge of tropical diseases. They both helped these early European colonies and rebelled against them, contributing to this rich history in the New World. American history is Native American, European, African, and world history.

Comparing and Contrasting the Original Colonies

The Thirteen Original Colonies that comprised British colonial America had unique characteristics. The New England Colonies (Massachusetts, Connecticut, Rhode Island, and New Hampshire) are all located in the northeastern region of the United States. Their economies relied on subsistence farming, fishing, shipbuilding, and trade. The New England colonists were mostly Puritans and self-governing through town meetings. Harvard University was founded in Cambridge, Massachusetts in 1636. No other religious faction had more influence over the eventual founding of the United States or continues to influence US foreign policy more than the Puritans.

The Puritans and the New England Colonies

The Puritans have been characterized as sulking, repressive, and fun hating. Social critic H.L. Menken once wrote, "Puritanism is the haunting fear that someone, somewhere, may be happy."

In many ways, we could look back at the Puritans and see people who opposed free-thinking, religious liberty, and democratic government. It appeared that they, in essence, created theocracies in New England. However, let us think historically and put them into the context of their times. They stood for religious liberty and democracy, breaking from the oppressive English regime. Strict controls on their towns may have resulted more from a harsh environment that demanded cooperation for joint survival. The clergy founded schools that stimulated education. So, on balance, the Puritans were repressive but relatively liberated compared to other societies within the context of their historical time. They provided a baseline for future academic intellectuals like Ralph Waldo Emerson, Henry David Thoreau, and Nathaniel Hawthorne, all influenced by Puritan values such as thrift, hard work, moral earnestness, and social responsibility. It might be worthwhile to look at the origins of Puritanism since it has influenced who we are as Americans.

To understand Puritanism, you must approach the Protestant Reformation led by a German monk named Martin Luther in 1517. What was he protesting, you might ask? Well, he believed that the Catholic Church was selling forgiveness and that good works and support for the church alone did not guarantee salvation. His point was that a person could be saved only through a personal relationship with God. This relies upon individualism and does not require a priest, church, or government mediation. Henry VIII replaced the Church of Rome with the Church of England in the 16th century so he could divorce his wife but retained much of the Catholic hierarchy style (i.e., bishops, archbishops, the rituals). The Puritans wanted a purer form of Protestantism, leading to their persecution in England and subsequent escape to the Americas.

The Pilgrims were the most extreme and uncompromising sect of Puritans. As noted in the previous chapter, the Pilgrims were heading to Virginia when they were blown off course and ended up in Cape Cod in 1620. The Plymouth Colony they formed set the stage for future government structure in America. Although nearly half of them died and their numbers were small (ultimately never more than 7000), their influence is still felt today. Their journey to America started the process of becoming less English and establishing a unique American identity. Harvard College was established in 1636 to train Puritan ministers when only 50% of men were literate and only 25% of women.

New England towns were tightly grouped, with no family getting more room than they needed. Families in New England lived under harsh discipline with forced perfection (sometimes, children were even brought to court). Fishing was the most significant industry in addition to lumber, shipping, and trading. The Yankee Merchant Marine was the biggest of all the colonies. Politics and religion were closely intertwined, with the meeting house serving as a city hall and a church. Massachusetts Bay Colony leader John Winthrop described the colony in his famous "Model of Christian Charity" sermon in 1630.

"For we must consider that we shall be as a city upon a hill. The eyes of all people are upon us."

Derivations of that John Winthrop phrase are still used by American politicians today to call out American exceptionalism and responsibility in the world. Winthrop took the phrase from Jesus's Sermon on the Mount revealed in Matthew 5:14.

"You are the light of the world. A city on a hill cannot be hidden."

To shine a spotlight on one Puritan colonist and to illustrate how life was for women in the Puritan colonies, it would be advantageous to examine the life of Ann Hutchinson. She arrived in the Massachusetts Bay Colony in September 1634. Within three years, she was branded a heretic, excommunicated from the church, and banished from the colony. Ann had come to New England as a follower of John

Cotton, who preached the covenant of grace rather than works. She began to hold weekly meetings in her home after his sermons so her friends could continue discussions. Although it was not uncommon to hold separate meetings, she then began to develop her independent ideas, which brought the attention of the Massachusetts Bay Colony Governor John Winthrop. Hutchinson interpreted the covenant of grace, meaning that only God gives the gift of grace and salvation, not the church, and there was nothing you could do to buy your way into heaven. This contradicted the widespread belief that behavior, ethics, and good works could bring salvation. Ann argued that the relationship with God was personal and did not require intermediaries. She also professed that men and women were equal before God. After her banishment, she moved to Rhode Island and was killed by Native Americans in 1643.

Figure 3.1: Ann Hutchinson on Trial

Dear readers, with your indulgence, I would like to share my experience at a job interview in New Hampshire. I must warn you, however, that it is a ghost story—first, some background. New Hampshire was established as a colony in 1623 by Captain John Mason and Sir Ferdinando Gorges, and the first permanent settlement was at Hilton's Point (now Dover). Many of the early colonists in New Hampshire were Puritans, like those in the Massachusetts Bay and Plymouth Colonies, where they played significant roles in establishing the social, religious, and political structures of the colonies.

My experience was in New London, New Hampshire, 75 miles west of the original colonial settlement. The town was settled permanently in 1779.

I went on a job interview at Colby-Sawyer College in the spring of 1999. The college is in New London, New Hampshire. I flew directly from Los Angeles to Boston and then took a bus from Boston to New London. When I was dropped off on the highway near the town, I was met by a fellow professor who would serve as my host while I was visiting. As we drove into New London, I noticed how old it was, a typical New England town, like in a Stephen King novel. It was rather spooky because the trees were barren of leaves as it was April and early enough in the spring for some lingering patches of snow here and there. Expecting to be taken to a hotel in town, I was surprised when we instead pulled up to an old building, possibly from the early 1800s. It stood alone on a large plot of land surrounded by a few twisted, leafless trees.

"What's this building?" I asked.

"Oh, this is the Old Academy Building. We use it for our out-of-town guests," he said.

"It's old and beautiful," I said. At that point, I figured that others would also be staying there. A shiver ran down my spine as we pulled up and parked in the back of the building. I grabbed my bags as my host stuck a skeleton key in a rusty lock on the heavy wooden door, and then we walked up the creaky wooden staircase to the second floor. The long-standing building had a musty smell but was in excellent condition. My room was the corner bedroom. It was filled with antiques and had what I would call a tall grandma bed. My host told me he would pick me up in the morning, or I could meet him at the administration office on campus if I wanted to walk (it was a short quarter-mile walk). I told him I didn't need a ride and would enjoy walking. Finally, I had to ask.

"Where are the other guests?"

"Oh, you're the only one," he said matter-of-factly, then left quickly. After he had pulled away, I began to feel very alone. The wind was blowing outside and making eerie whistling noises. It was starting to get dark. I began to unpack my suitcase and was thinking about my teaching demonstration that would be part of my interview the next day. Then, after a few minutes, I went into the bathroom to brush my teeth and wash my face. I felt uneasy as I stood over the sink as if someone were watching me. The faucet and all fixtures were antique and in superb condition. Then I decided to look around a bit. The upstairs had accommodation for six guests. All the guest rooms were equally splendid regarding antiques and general condition. The large upstairs meeting room had a gallery of old portraits on the walls and many long wooden tables and chairs. Most of the portraits were of dour old New Englanders, which I chose not to examine closely. I returned to my room and read *The Tin Drum* by Günter Grass. Then I heard what seemed like creaking noises from the wooden floors. I dismissed this as just settling noises common in many old wooden buildings. Then I heard distinct footsteps downstairs on the wood floor and a faint human voice. I figured my host had come back to check on me. I stood up, walked to the top of the staircase, and called out.

"Hello. Is anybody there? No response. I called out again.

"Hello, is somebody there?" I did not receive a response. I then returned to my room and started reading again, thinking my imagination was getting the best of me. Then I heard more voices and chairs moving and sliding about on the wood floor downstairs. I got up and investigated but saw no one, and the sounds had stopped. I was feeling thoroughly spooked at this point. On my flip phone, I called my wife, Heather, and told her what was happening.

"Get out! Right now, get out!" she pleaded.

"I can't. It's dark, and the guy who's my host has gone home. I'm here all by myself. I have nowhere to go. Besides," I told her, "I don't want to seem like a wimp." She thought I was crazy.

I hung up, returned to my room, and sat on my bed very uneasily. I tried to take my mind off these peculiar sounds by reading more, but there was no let-up. The voices started again; many more were coming from downstairs. It was as if a party was going on. Chairs were sliding, footsteps were on the wooden floorboards, and the voices continued. I got under the covers and pulled them up tight to my chin, hunkered down for what would undoubtedly be a long night. At that point, I heard an old Victrola playing music downstairs. There were more voices, more chairs moving, and more creaky footsteps. I sprang up from my bed.

"Stop. Stop it now!" I cried out. I went halfway down the staircase to investigate. By that time, the noises and music had stopped. I called my wife again and wanted to document that I wasn't crazy or dreaming.

"Get out!" she kept repeating. Then I climbed back upstairs and went to bed. I slept lightly, with one eye open all night, as the noises randomly continued intermittently.

The following day, I woke up and ventured out of the old building to find some breakfast, but nothing was open. I wandered the streets and looked at all the quaint shops until I finally saw another living soul—a street sweeper. He wore dark woolen clothing and had a very traditional straw broom. He greeted me in his New England accent.

"Morning friend, what are you doing in town?" he asked.

"I'm here for a job interview at the college," I said. The street sweeper looked at me, smiling.

"Is that so? Where are you staying, if you don't mind me asking?" he asked. I turned around and pointed at the Old Academy Building.

"Up there, in the Old Academy Building," I said.

"You're lucky; not many folks get to stay there. Did they tell you it's haunted?" he asked casually. I laughed nervously.

"No, no one told me, and I did have some odd experiences last night," I said.

"It's one of the most haunted places in New England," he said with pride.

"Is that a fact?" I asked.

"Yup. Last week, they brought a lady in for an interview and put her in the Old Academy Building. Well, I'll tell you, in the middle of the night, she could take no more of it and ran out into the street screaming for help. They were able to put her in a hotel in town," he said with a smile.

"I can understand for sure. Well, I made it, but just barely," I remarked.

"Good luck to you, friend," he said, shaking my hand.

"Thank you. Have a good day," I said as he walked away to continue his street-sweeping duties. I finally found a coffee shop and got some coffee and a sweet roll for breakfast. I read the local paper and waited. At long last, it came time for me to walk up the hill to the college administration office and meet my host. He greeted me.

"How did you sleep last night? Was everything okay?" he asked. I looked at him carefully for a clue as to his intentions.

"Splendid," I lied, not elaborating on what had happened. I figured that perhaps the haunted building was part of the interview process. We attended various meetings with deans, other administrators, and fellow teachers. They didn't ask, and I didn't tell them what had happened the previous night. After that, a formal hiring board interrogated me for nearly an hour. It was then time for lunch. I had a pleasant lunch with the student body president and some student government officers. We met in the cafeteria.

"Where are you staying?" the bubbly young girl who was the student body president asked.

"The Old Academy Building," I said.

"Wow, I want to stay there," she said.

"Me too," said another girl.

"Yeah, we all want to stay there, but no one's allowed," another girl said.

"This whole college is haunted, but the academy building is the most haunted place," said the student body president.

"So, I'm told," I said.

"At least you made it through the night, not like the last person they tried to interview," one of the other students said.

"Well, I want this job, and I figured it was just part of the interview process," I said with a smile. The students all laughed.

"Hey, I heard Leonard Nimoy and the film crew from *In Search of...* came here in the late 1970s to film a special episode," added one of the girls.

"Was it *that* show? I thought it was that other one," said another student.

After lunch, it was time for my teaching demonstration. There were some technical difficulties, and it was delayed for nearly two hours. My host suggested I take advantage of the downtime to visit the library and look around. I decided to do some research.

Colby-Sawyer College was founded in 1837 when a legislative charter was granted to eleven New London citizens to establish a school in the town. In May of 1838, the academy welcomed its first students. Susan Colby served as the first teacher and principal. She later married James B. Colgate of New York but remained actively involved with the school's progress. This unique relationship with the Colby family was formally recognized in 1878 when the New London Academy was renamed Colby Academy. Many people have reported strange paranormal events in the building. Most of these reports came from professors who used the building as temporary housing overnight when they were snowed in at the college.

After nearly two hours, my host came to the library to retrieve me. It was time for my teaching demonstration. It all went well, and it was time to meet the college president. I thought that maybe now they would acknowledge that they had put me in a haunted building to test me and then offer me the job because of my steely nerves and perseverance—no such luck. There was no mention of the haunted building and no immediate job offer.

After the meeting with the college president, my host met me outside the president's office.

"How did it go today?" asked my host.

"Oh, fine, it went well; I'm tired and ready to go home, though," I said. My host winced a little.

"I'm sorry, but you missed the last bus back to Boston. You'll have to go tomorrow morning. I can put you up in the Old Academy Building again tonight," he said.

I was devastated. Oh, great. It was another night in that spooky old building. What choice did I have? Could I confess my fear and perhaps blow my chances for a job? Or should I tough it out and risk dying from fright? We walked to my host's car, and I got in. We drove back down the hill. Another chill ran down my spine as we went to the haunted building and parked around the back.

"I'll see you bright and early. Sleep well," he said, probably knowing full well that I wouldn't.

"OK, thanks. Good night," I said unenthusiastically. As he drove away, I began to hear every creak in that building. Would the second night be worse than the first? I knew only one thing for sure—I was not alone.

It was growing dark and gloomy. There was no moon, and it was overcast. The wind was picking up, and I could hear an eerie whistling sound coming from the eaves of the old, haunted building. Dead leaves rustled on the ground and swirled around the gnarly old trees. I would have to survive one more night and get a ride at seven o'clock the following day.

I hunkered down for the evening again, being the only guest in the Old Academy building. I was ready for sleep and hoped it would be restful this time.

Not long after I laid down, the sounds began again. First, there were voices, then chairs sliding, and then footsteps on the wooden floor downstairs. And then, if that wasn't bad enough, that damn Victrola started playing again. It got louder and louder and louder. I pulled the covers over my head. Then I heard footsteps starting up the creaky wooden stairs; I could listen to them approaching me. *Oh God, will I make it tonight*? I thought. I resigned myself to the possibility that the cacophony of noises was probably leading to a crescendo event that I could only, in my worst nightmares, imagine. Then, suddenly, all was quiet and still. I peeked out from under my covers and saw the room before me; a faint light was coming from a single bulb in the stairway that caused the creepy antique furniture in my room to cast eerie shadows. I breathed a heavy sigh of relief. A few minutes passed, and I began to settle a bit.

Then she came. A ghostly visage suddenly appeared in the corner of my room by the windows—an old woman in a black dress and bonnet. I was so frightened that I could feel my heart beating in my eyes. She was grim-faced and had her arms folded across her chest. She wasn't happy. She just hovered there, not entirely transparent, but nearly so. She said nothing. My heart was beating so fast I could barely breathe, and I couldn't move. After probably only a few minutes, but it seemed like hours, she went away. It was quiet and uneventful for the rest of the night. I finally fell asleep, emotionally drained and physically exhausted.

I woke up the following day and was thankful to be alive. As I packed my things, I decided to have one last look around. I looked at the gallery of portraits again, and suddenly, my heart stopped. There she was: Susan Colby, the founder of the college. Its first president and teacher. It was she who appeared in ghostly form in my room the night before. I stared at the portrait as her penetrating eyes paralyzed me temporarily. I then heard my host drive up the driveway, and I left the haunted building behind. My trip home was uneventful, and a week later, I found out I didn't get the job.

Since my visit, the college has donated the original New London Academy Building to the town of New London. It has been refurbished and serves as the community's town hall. Stories of strange happenings and ghosts are still being reported at the site.

Figure 3.2: Old Academy Building

The Middle Colonies

The Middle Colonies (New York, New Jersey, Pennsylvania, and Delaware) were situated on the upper mid-Atlantic coast, south of New England. Their diverse economies included agriculture (wheat, corn, and livestock), trade, and some manufacturing. The Middle Colonies had Quakers, Catholics, and Dutch Reformed Church members governed by representative assemblies. Philadelphia became a trading hub and the center of William Penn's Quaker "Holy Experiment." The Dutch and Swedes initially settled in the Middle Colonies, but they developed little of the land. England got New York from the Netherlands by conquering New Netherland in 1664.

In May 1664, an expeditionary force with four warships and about 300 soldiers arrived on Long Island. The British offered the Dutch lenient terms of surrender, which they eventually accepted. New Amsterdam was renamed New York City, and the English peacefully captured the rest of New Netherland (changed to New York). In 1673, the Dutch temporarily recaptured New York, but with the Treaty of Westminster signed one year later, the colony returned to British hands.

New Jersey broke away from New York in 1738, and Pennsylvania was given to William Penn by Charles II. Delaware was taken from the Swedes in 1664. Ultimately, all these colonies were set up to make profits for Great Britain. Most settlers arrived with families, and Quakers went to Pennsylvania. The population of the Middle Colonies boomed because the settlers had families already. With large families, a growing population, shipbuilding, ironworks, trading and shipping, and lumber, the Middle Colonies expanded rapidly and became the most urbanized of the three colonial regions. Slowly, the colonial legislatures began to usurp power from the British colonial governor. Great Britain formed the Board of Trade to reestablish control, but their efforts failed.

The Southern Colonies

The Southern Colonies included Maryland, Virginia, North Carolina, South Carolina, and Georgia. They all boasted warm climates and had an abundance of rich, fertile soil for farming. The economies of the Southern Colonies were dominated by large plantations, and slave labor was used to produce cash crops like tobacco, rice, and indigo. The dominant religion among the southern colonists was Anglican (Church of England). As noted, the first permanent English colony was in Jamestown, Virginia, where less than half the colonists survived the first year. The Virginia Company, to entice others to come, offered new colonists free land after seven years of indentured servitude. They were an unruly and undisciplined people, and anarchy soon ensued. There was starvation and even cannibalism (reportedly, one man ate his wife). The chances for success were minimal, and colonists constantly faced the threat of hostile Native Americans.

Southern colonial towns were spread out, unlike New England. This led to social isolation. However, the Southern Colonies became an economic force for colonial America as the fertile soil helped bring significant profits from tobacco, rice, and silk. The settlers in the South generally did not bring their families with them as they were focused on economic gain. There was religious practice in the South, but the churches were farther apart, and people were more tolerant than the New Englanders, even allowing gambling. Food also played a significant role in their lives. Almost everyone in the Southern Colonies lived on plantations that were the heart of the economy. Like the Middle Colonies, most commodities, such as agricultural goods, were sold to England. Slavery was instrumental in the economic success of the Southern Colonies, which would not have been possible without it. Tobacco was the most important crop, with the peak tobacco boom being from 1618 to 1629, fueled by tremendous demand in England. In the Carolinas, rice was the most lucrative crop. Rice especially required intensive care in cultivation, and slave labor was considered essential. Enslaved Africans had extensive knowledge of growing crops and natural immunity to malaria and were used to working under hot and humid conditions. The economic success prompted an insatiable demand for labor, both indentured and slave.

Cecilius Calvert, the Lord of Baltimore, a friend of Charles I of England, was granted 12 million acres of land at the tip of Chesapeake Bay in 1632. The area was named Maryland in tribute to Queen Mary. Calvert hoped to create a haven for Catholics to live harmoniously with Protestants. Maryland prospered as a tobacco colony, but most of the colonists in Maryland were Protestants who had relocated from Virginia. Eventually, Calvert lost control, and Maryland became a royal colony. Religion was the primary factor for the establishment of other colonies as well, including the New England Colonies of Connecticut and Rhode Island.

Bacon's Rebellion

The Southern Colonies boasted the first elected assembly in the English Colonies. Virginia's House of Burgesses (1619) and the Governor's Council (1650) provided governance, although it was not democratic as the council members served for life. Under such management, Virginia remained free from much trouble until a conflict broke out between Doeg Indians and Virginia farmers led by a wealthy Englishman named Nathaniel Bacon. This conflict became known as Bacon's Rebellion, an armed uprising in the Virginia Colony between 1676 and 1677.

The Governor of Virginia, William Berkeley, had built a string of defensive fortresses, but the farmers felt that was not enough and wanted to go on the offensive.

The rebellion's leader, Nathaniel Bacon, rallied supporters, including both Black and White indentured servants as well as African slaves. They opposed the policies of Colonial Governor William Berkeley and the wealthy plantation owners of East Virginia. The rebellion was sparked by tensions related to high taxes, falling tobacco prices, and escalating conflicts with Native Americans along the western frontier. Nathaniel Bacon requested that Governor Berkeley take action to drive Native American Indians out of Virginia. However, Berkeley refused, leading to the rebellion.

A group of three hundred farmers led by Bacon started a war with the Indians in April 1676. When Bacon died later that year, so too did the rebellion. Although the rebellion did not achieve its initial goal of expelling Native Americans from Virginia, it did result in Berkeley being recalled to England. The uprising also had a lasting impact on the use of slave labor in Virginia. It also revealed class differences in the early colonies and the need for a stronger central government.

There was solidification of the British North American colonies in the 17th century, but this process did not occur peacefully, as we have seen with Bacon's Rebellion. Other settlements were not immune to violence, including the Pequot War, the Mystic massacre, King Philip's War, and the Susquehannock War.

The Pequot War

The Pequot War (1636 to 1638) in New England was between the Pequot Tribe and an alliance of English settlers from Massachusetts Bay, Plymouth, and Saybrook Colonies, along with allied Narragansett and Mohegan Tribes. The war was ignited by the murder of a trader named John Stone at the hands of the Pequot Tribe. More than seven hundred Pequots were killed or captured, some of whom were sold into slavery. The Mystic or Pequot Massacre was a crucial event in the Pequot War. European colonists traded with all three tribes in their region (Pequot, Mohegan, and Narragansett), exchanging European goods for furs. In 1637, after the conflict had already begun, Pequot warriors attacked the village of Wethersfield, killing unarmed settlers. This came after a hurricane in 1635 that had damaged harvests leading to scarcities and more tension. On May 26, 1637, a paramilitary force from the Connecticut Colony, led by Captain John Mason, along with Native American allies who were hostile to the Pequot, attacked a Pequot village near the Mystic River. Captain Mason ordered that the town be put to the torch, which killed almost all the Pequot in the village.

The English victory culminated with the Treaty of Hartford in 1638. The Pequot War was the first war between the New England colonists and the Native Americans. The Mohegan tribe gained power and influence with the defeat of their rivals, the

Pequots, and eventually, they joined the Wampanoag in their war against the Puritans.

King Philip's War

King Philip's War was more destructive than the Pequot War and ultimately ended Native American power in New England. Between 1675 and 1676, the war was also known as the First Indian War, Metacom's War, or Metacom's Rebellion. The war was named after the Pokanoket chief of the Wampanoag Tribe, Metacom. He adopted the English name King Philip based on friendly relations his father had with the Plymouth Colony. Tensions between the colonists and the Native Americans rose when the colonies violated peace agreements dealing with guns and the execution of Wampanoags for murder. Tribal raiding parties attacked settlements in Massachusetts, Rhode Island, Connecticut, and Maine, which then led to counterattacks by the colonial militia and Native allies numbering over one thousand men. The war ended with the signing of the Treaty of Casco Bay in 1678, but relations between Native Americans and English settlers would never be the same.

The Susquehannock War

Yet another significant conflict between Native American tribes and European settlers along the East Coast was the Susquehannock War of 1676. The Susquehannock were an Iroquoian-speaking tribe that lived alongside the Susquehanna River in New York, Pennsylvania, and Maryland. The Susquehannock had been constantly at war with the Iroquois, who eventually defeated them in 1676. Epidemics and war significantly reduced their population.

These conflicts changed the political and demographic landscape of New England. Nearly 1000 English colonists and at least 3000 Native Americans died in these wars. Many others left or were sold into slavery. Native Americans comprised 25% of New England's population in 1670, but 10 years later, that had been reduced to 10%. The casualties and brutality on both sides created hatred that simmered well beyond the cessation of hostilities.

Salem Witch Trials

As if fear of war with the Native Americans was not enough, New Englanders also faced a new fear in the form of the supernatural, beginning in 1692 and ending a year later. Salem Town, Salem Village, Ipswich, and Andover all put women and men on trial for witchcraft. In the ensuing hysterical paranoia, 14 women and six men were executed, and five others died in prison. The trouble began during the spring of 1692 when a small group of young girls in Salem Village claimed to be possessed by the devil. They then accused some older local women of witchcraft, blaming them for their possession. This triggered an emotional wave of hysteria in the whole region. This was all based on the belief that the power of the devil could be summoned by witches who could use that power to harm or influence others, which was a common belief in Europe and throughout New England. Several of the young girls began to experience screaming fits and violent physical contortions. This then spread to other young girls in the community. The elders decided that three women were to blame: Tituba (a slave), Sarah Good (a beggar), and Sarah Osborn (an elderly woman). The girls all accused these three women of bewitching them and forcing the devil on them. Luckily, public opinion in the region turned against the accusers, and things settled down.

Figure 3.3: Salem Witch Trials

At this point, and as a way of summary, it would be prudent to compare and contrast the Original Thirteen Colonies to demonstrate their diversity.

Colony	Year	Reason	Leader(s)	Economy	Origin of Name
Massachusetts	1620	Religion	William Bradford and John Winthrop	Fishing, shipbuilding, lumber, trade, whaling	Indian name for Big Hill
New Hampshire	1623	Profit	Benning Wentworth, John Wentworth, John Wheelwright	Trade, fishing	Named after Hampshire, England
Connecticut	1636	Religion	Thomas Hooker	Trade	Indian name for long tidal river

Rhode Island	1636	Religion	Roger Williams	Shipping, livestock, farming	Disputed
New York	1625	Profit	James, Duke of York	Farming, fur trade, shipbuilding	Named after York in England
Delaware	1638	Profit	Peter Minuit	Trade, farming	English Lord of De La Ware
New Jersey	1664	Profit	John Berkeley, George Carteret	Trade, farming	Named after English island of Jersey
Pennsylvania	1637	Religion	William Penn	Trade, farming	Wooded lands
Virginia	1607	Profit	John Smith, John Rolfe	Tobacco	Named for Queen Elizabeth
Maryland	1632	Religion	George Calvert, Lord of Baltimore	Tobacco	Named for Queen Mary
North and South Carolina	1663	Profit	William Berkeley	Rice, indigo, tobacco	Named for King Charles
Georgia	1732	Penal colony	James Oglethorpe	Rice, indigo, trade, livestock	Named for King George

Figure 3.4: Comparing and Contrasting the Original Thirteen Colonies

As you can see from the chart, the New England Colonies relied on trade and shipbuilding, while the Middle Colonies developed diverse agricultural economies. The Southern Colonies mainly relied on cash crops. New England was predominantly Puritan and strict, while the Middle Colonies had religious diversity and tolerance, and the Southern Colonies were primarily Anglican (Church of England) and somewhat more tolerant than the Puritans. In terms of government, New England had town meetings and self-governance, while the Middle and Southern Colonies had representative assemblies. Climate-wise, New England had severe winters, the Middle Colonies shared a moderate climate, and the climate in the Southern Colonies was mild and warm. Lastly, as for the workforce, New England relied on family labor, while the Middle Colonies had a mix of family and hired labor, and the Southern Colonies relied mainly on enslaved Africans.

Slavery

Whether you say that it began in 1619 or 1526 or whether Spain, Portugal, or Great Britain is to blame, slavery is at the center of America's story of both economic success and moral failure. The American colonies emerged in a whirlwind of ambition, religious fervor, greed, curiosity, adventure, cruelty, and barbarity. Native Americans witnessed an unstoppable force take and use their land and resources with no understanding or appreciation of the sacred connection the Native people had to the Earth and the cosmos. As a unique American society developed, race-based chattel slavery increasingly defined the colonial economy and that of the British Empire. The British thought of the American colonies as sleepy backwaters compared to the wealth-producing Caribbean islands where sugar was king. However, these more extensive transatlantic economic trading networks connected America to the world, eventually bringing the colonists into conflict with Great Britain.

Race-based slavery, at the scale of the transatlantic slave trade, was something new in world history. Before the emergence of this evil business, one could find African kings and queens visiting the crowned heads of Europe, as evidenced by painted portraits. There was no immediate categorization or discrimination by race; that was something that slavery on a global scale would unleash on our world. The first justification was profit. Captain Thomas Phillips, the Master of a slave ship in 1694, explained his simple justification in his journal (*Voyage of the Hannibal, 1694*):

"I can't think there is any intrinsic value in one color more than another, nor that white is better than black, only we think it so because we are so."

Captain Phillips also writes about dealing with an African king in the process of buying slaves. The process was transactional, with little regard for race. The English colonies had a problem: lots of land and insufficient labor. Portuguese, Dutch, and English ships became the pipeline for slave labor from Africa. Most slaves embarked upon the Middle Passage on the west coast of Africa. Raiding parties and conflict between the people of Africa produced captives who could be sold on the coast to slave traders for beads, cloth, rum, firearms, and metal wares. So, it is true that Black Africans sold other Black Africans into slavery, but that does not excuse the institution of slavery or absolve others from any guilt, shame, or blame.

After greed and profit, the following justification for enslaving Black Africans came from a religious distinction. In other words, it was okay to enslave non-Christians. When the slaves began to adopt Christianity, then the concept of skin color was used as a determinant. There was too much money and power at stake. The Bible (Timothy 6:10) notes that money is the root of all evil, which certainly applies in this case. By the 1660s, new laws were enacted that codified the status of Black slaves.

Native Americans who were captured in the many wars with the colonists were also sold into slavery. The justification for such slavery was not necessarily race but greed for land and wanting to remove the Native people from the land and thereby quell the rebellion against further settlement. The Native Americans sent to the Caribbean did not last long and were not profitable enough for the enslavers. A more stable and resilient slave workforce was needed, and that is where the demand for African slaves comes into the picture.

European slave ships brought millions of Africans across the Atlantic Ocean on a torturous journey known as the Middle Passage. The ships were packed tight, with little consideration given to the chained Africans who suffered unimaginable hardship. The Africans were subject to beatings, rapes, malnourishment, disease, lack of fresh air, and lack of any medical care. Some committed suicide by jumping overboard to escape their enslavers. To better understand the horrors of the Middle Passage, I would suggest watching the movie *Amistad.* Approximately 15% of the shackled slaves died on the voyage, with 10.7 million arriving in the Caribbean.

Middle Passage comes from the three legs of the journey from Africa to the Americas. The first leg was the overland journey from the interior of Africa to the coastal slave-trading fortress. The second leg was the sea journey to the Caribbean islands, where the slave ships would drop off their chained human cargo and take on sugar and other goods from the Americas. The third leg of the journey was the "seasoning" the African slaves would endure on the sugar plantations before being sold to plantations in the Americas. By far, the most significant number of slaves ended up in Brazil. About 450,000 Africans landed in North America, changing the destiny of the English colonies.

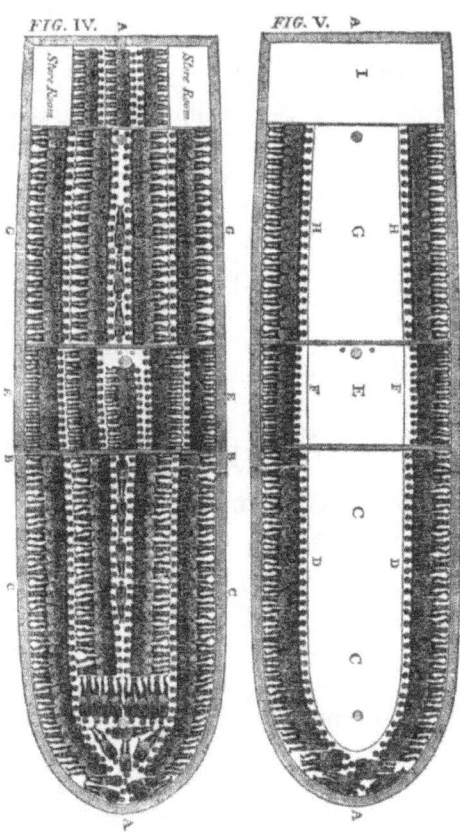

Figure 3.5: Slave Ship Diagram

Conclusion

By the end of the seventeenth century, Great Britain's North American colonies had developed and matured. The colonists were organized and driven by conflict: the environment, interference from England, Native Americans, and even with each other. They accepted entrance into a transatlantic economy based on slavery and began the process of separation from their homeland politically, economically, culturally, socially, and spiritually. As diverse as they were, the colonies were taking on a unique identity. By 1763, American colonists were uniting and seeing themselves as not full British subjects. They began to see England as more of a threat than a protector. The Stamp Act of 1765 caused the Americans to cooperate against English taxes. It led to boycotts of British goods and began to stitch together a shared narrative of liberty, sacrifice, and resistance. A rebellion was brewing as a uniquely American nationalism was stirring.

Recommended Sources

Colonial America: New World Settlements. https://www.history.com/topics/colonial-america.

Colonial Settlement, 1600s–1763. https://www.loc.gov/classroom-materials/united-states-history-primary-source-timeline/colonial-settlement-1600-1763/.

Charles Johnson. *Middle Passage.*

Credits

Figure 3.1: Ann Hutchinson on Trial. Source: https://www.jssgallery.org/Other_Artists/Edwin_Austin_Abbey/Anne_Hutchinson_on_Trial.htm.

Figure 3.2: Old Academy Building. Source: Illustration by Gary Dumm in *Timeless: A Paranormal Personal History* by Bruce Olav Solheim.

Figure 3.3: Salem Witch Trials. Source: https://commons.wikimedia.org/wiki/File:Salem_witch2_courtesy_copy.jpg.

Figure 3.4: Comparing and Contrasting the Original Thirteen Colonies. Source: The author.

Figure 3.5: Slave Ship Diagram. Source: https://commons.wikimedia.org/wiki/File:Slave_ship_diagram.png.

CHAPTER FOUR

Revolutionizing America

> Objectives
> 1. Discover the origins of the American Revolution.
> 2. Identify the reasons why the colonies were able to defeat Great Britain.
> 3. Comprehend the impact and legacy of the American Revolution.
> 4. Understand the distinct roles played by the Founding Fathers.

"His problem is that he doesn't know his place." A senior college administrator once said that about me at an academic dean's meeting. One of the deans in attendance told me this later in confidence. I suppose it was intended to be mean, but it sounded more like frustration on his part. I had gone over his head and that of my dean to talk directly to the college president and start a unique distance education program for the US Navy that proved to be remarkably successful. I consider his statement to be a great compliment. I am glad that I have the freedom not to know my place. Where would this country be if everyone stayed in their place and tacitly accepted what others told them or expected of them? None of our American heroes were such timid creatures. President Barack Obama authored a book entitled: *The Audacity of Hope*. I believe not only in the audacity of hope but in the audacity of purpose and action. As Georges Danton, a leader in the initial stages of the French Revolution, wrote in 1792: *"L'audace, l'audace, toujours l'audace."* Or, in English, "Audacity, audacity, always audacity."

It is almost cliché to hear people say: "speak truth to power." But how many people do just that? Few, I would suspect. I have always held that the truth is the truth, no matter how uncomfortable it may be. I want to know the truth, and I suspect deep down inside, so does everyone else. So, what is it that stops us from pursuing the truth? Answer: Fear. I, for one, am tired of living in fear. We must liberate ourselves from the conventions and constraints of the past and adopt a bold new vision. American patriot Patrick Henry wrote in 1775, "I know not what course others may take; but as for me, give me liberty, or give me death!"

Patrick Henry was not kidding around. What is this life worth living for if you are not living it freely and truthfully? So, dear reader, it is okay to be different, to think differently, and to live your own true, authentic life as you sense it in every possible way. To do otherwise is not to be honest. As we grow older, we realize that we are all the heroes of our own life story and truly embrace the whole meaning of

Shakespeare's words, "to thine own self be true." Indeed, it comes down to this, I do not know my place, and neither should you.

Origins of the American Revolution

In a letter to Hezekiah Niles on February 13, 1818, Founding Father John Adams wrote:

"The Revolution was effected before the War commenced. The Revolution was in the Minds and Hearts of the People. A Change in their Religious Sentiments of their Duties and Obligations."

This shift of allegiance from England to America took place between 1760 and 1775. To understand this shift, we must look at the impact of the Seven Years War, 1756–1763 (the French and Indian War in North America). France was losing power in North America. The colonists met in the Albany Congress in 1754 to address the French threat. The French and Indian War started with a foolhardy attack by George Washington, who served as a colonel in the Virginia Regiment.

Colonel Washington took on the French at Fort Duquesne (now Pittsburgh). In 1754, he ordered his forces to construct Fort Necessity near the contested Ohio River Valley. The French were aware of what he was doing, so they sent their forces (French troops and Indian allies) to attack Washington's forces, who were outnumbered and in a vulnerable location. After only one day of fighting, George Washington was forced to surrender. The defeat impacted his military reputation, but Washington did learn from his mistakes. His attack on the French was impulsive and poorly planned. From his failure, he learned the importance of strategic positioning, intelligence gathering, and disciplined decision-making. These lessons he implemented later during the American Revolutionary War. The incident escalated tensions between the English and French in America, leading to a broader global war (The Seven Years' War).

Figure 4.1: John Adams

The Seven Years' War became a global conflict involving many European powers. Great Britain and Prussia were on one side, and France, Spain, Saxony, Sweden, and Russia were on the other. Ultimately, France ceded its North American territories east of the Mississippi River, Canada, and other possessions to England. Spain obtained Louisiana and French territory west of the Mississippi. They also got Florida from Great Britain. The Seven Years' War profoundly impacted the global balance of power. It provided the colonies in America an opportunity to gain more autonomy as the Treaty of Paris in 1763 removed France from North America and left Great Britain grappling with managing its sprawling world empire.

The New England and British soldiers fought together in the French and Indian War, but there were tensions. The Native Americans could no longer play the British and French against each other, and the Americans no longer feared the French at their borders. The turning point came in 1763 when Great Britain raised taxes on the colonies to help reduce its heavy war debt from the Seven Years' War. The British Proclamation of 1763 was intended to prevent future conflict with the Native tribes, but it also prevented American colonial expansion. A broad coalition of American colonists resisted new British taxation.

The role of King George III of England in the American Revolution is subject to debate. Was he to blame, partly to blame, or blameless? He was indeed young, mediocre, and a poor judge of character. Due to his inexperience, he was overly dependent on older advisors. Thomas Jefferson blamed King George, but the British ministries made poor decisions, causing disaffection and rebellion in the colonies, and we cannot forget that the colonists themselves were already moving away from the notion of being English before any of these official actions. King George advocated stronger measures because he believed England had been too lenient, but he alone was not responsible for the rift.

The Stamp, Declaratory, and Townsend Acts

The Stamp Act required a royal stamp on all printed materials. The ensuing crisis brought the lower economic classes into politics and turned them against England. American merchants organized nonimportation agreements to pressure British exporters. Then, in 1766, the British Parliament passed the Declaratory Act, which asserted its right to tax and directly legislate over the American colonies. A year later, in 1767, the Townsend Acts levied taxes on paper, glass, and tea. These were taxes only on items imported from England. The purpose was to raise revenue to support the empire and control the colonies. The cost of maintaining a global empire doubled the national debt. England spent a great deal on security for the western frontiers of the North American colonies. All of this led England to gain more control over its North American colonies, which, in turn, led to resistance. The Royal Proclamation of 1763 stopped settlement west of the Appalachian Mountains, hoping to curtail the cost of securing the frontier. The colonists resented the move because they felt entitled to the territory since they fought alongside the British in the French and Indian War. The Sugar Act in 1764 was designed to stop the smuggling of molasses into New England, and the Currency Act restricted the colonies from producing paper money (gold and silver coins were hard to come by in Colonial America). This restriction made it hard for the colonies to function in a transatlantic economy. The Stamp Act (1765) and Sugar Act (1764) were the first direct taxes on the colonies. These two acts impacted a broad spectrum of colonial society and led to widespread resistance to England.

Colonial newspapers began to print stories of resistance, making people think they were part of the movement. Then, Great Britain sent its military to Boston in 1768 to help enforce the new acts and squash the resistance. On March 5, 1770, a crowd gathered outside the Custom House and began throwing things at the British sentries until the soldiers fired. Five Bostonians were killed, including Crispus Attucks, a former slave and dockworker. Oddly, John Adams defended the British soldiers and won their case. The incident became known as the Boston Massacre. A sense of shared grievance against England emerged from the British attempts to control the colonies, which slowly began to form an American political identity.

The Great Awakening: Religious Causes of the Revolution

There were religious causes to the American Revolution as well. The First Great Awakening began in the 1730s. Christian ministers had started to notice a drop in church attendance. Two ministers, Jonathan Edwards and George Whitefield, realized that they needed to stir things up to grow their flocks of parishioners. They broke from the dry, boring liturgies and encouraged an emotional response. At the same time, the Enlightenment, a European philosophical movement, was crossing the Atlantic and influencing the American colonists. Enlightenment thinkers preferred a scientific and logical view to a religious one. Many Christians noticed that pursuing wealth and rationalism were squeezing religion and spiritual worship out of everyday life, foreshadowing disunity. The colonies were already diverse in terms of religion. New England had its Puritan congregational churches. The Middle Colonies had a mixture of Anglicans, Lutherans, Baptists, Presbyterians, Dutch Reformed, and Congregational parishioners. The Southern colonies mainly consisted of Anglicans and Baptists, with some Presbyterians and Quakers.

At the end of the 1720s, a religious revival movement began with Jonathan Edwards, an Anglican minister, leading the charge. He preached that humans are sinners, and God is an angry judge. He said faith alone was enough and emphasized that people should ask for forgiveness. His most famous sermon, filled with emotionalism, "Sinners in the Hands of an Angry God," had a significant impact throughout the colonies. Another minister, George Whitefield, also picked up on the revivalist movement and converted many people to Protestantism. The Great Awakening forever changed American Christianity and culture and united the colonists throughout America—the first such uniting experience for the Thirteen Colonies. It impacted politics as well because colonists realized that religious power was in their own hands, so therefore, it made sense that political power was as well, and not in the hands of the British monarch. So, although all colonists did not share the same religious beliefs in 1775, they did share a common vision of freedom from British control. The Great Awakening created a political climate that made the American Revolution possible.

Social Causes of the Revolution

Sic semper tyrannis is a Latin phrase that means "thus be it to tyrants." In the build up to and during the American Revolution, the Founding Fathers used the phrase to encourage the American colonists in their fight for independence. In 1776, Virginia incorporated the phrase into their state seal. The words resonated with most American colonists, especially the middle and lower economic classes.

The middle-class colonists supported the revolution based on their dislike of the aristocracy. The Founding Fathers frequently used terminology like abject slavery, tyranny, and independence to build up the resistance to British rule. Phrases like "all men are created equal," which made their way into the Declaration of Independence, spoke to these commonly held sentiments. This points to the psychological underpinnings of the American colonists' decision to go to war.

Political Causes of the Revolution

Many colonists did not believe in a strong central government and were distrustful of it, so they favored more localized power. The fact that England was flexing its political muscles in America did not sit well with the colonists. The Founding Fathers believed in separating from England, but some still favored a strong central government, just not English. This led to the Federalist versus Anti-Federalist debates which still rage today (Federalists believe in a strong central government, and Anti-Federalists believe in states' rights). Ideologically, the colonists were ready to separate if not already separated from England.

Economic Causes of the Revolution

Most historians point to the colonists' desire for true independence of economic development without British interference as a major cause of the American Revolution. Indeed, the complaint of "no taxation without representation" alerts us to the colonists' disapproval of British tax authority and lack of a colonial voice in Parliament. England saw the colonies primarily as a source of revenue vital to paying for the European wars. Dear reader, in my study of American foreign policy (which is essentially a study of America's wars), I have found that Americans go to war if three underlying pre-conditions and reasons are present: economic, ideological, and psychological. As we have seen, the American colonists were ready to take on England based on satisfying the three conditions for war.

The Revolutionary War

A relatively weak and primarily divided group of colonies took on the most powerful nation on Earth and won. How was that possible? How did the American colonies prevail? We can start by looking at each side's strengths and weaknesses. Great Britain had a population of 7.5 million versus the American colonies, which had a population of only 2.5 million. England had a tremendous amount of wealth, and the colonies had little. Great Britain had the most powerful navy in the world, and the colonies had no official navy. The British had a professional army with 50,000 British soldiers, 30,000 German Hessian mercenaries, and 30,000 American loyalists. England did, however, have some disadvantages. There was unrest in Ireland, their government was inept and far away from the colonies, and King George, let's face it, was not a genius. Also, despite the British wanting to teach the Americans a lesson, there was some softheartedness for the colonists. There were military problems. The British had second-rate generals who treated their soldiers atrociously and provided little in the way of provisions. The British knew they needed a clear and quick victory to put the Americans in their place, which served to the advantage of the colonists, who could drag out the war on their home territory. The British Army was 3000 miles from home, and it took months for orders to be received from London. The Americans could strike quickly with independent initiative or could take their time and were able to run and hide in the vast amount of territory that England hoped to subdue.

Among the strengths of the colonists was that Americans had outstanding leadership, especially George Washington, who had learned some hard lessons from his failures in the French and Indian War. There was also the bonus of Benjamin Franklin's diplomatic cleverness and help from the French. The French general Marquis de La Fayette commanded American continental troops and was the hero of the decisive siege of Yorktown in 1781. The colonists fought a defensive war and were self-sustaining. Americans were also better marksmen than the British and had a moral advantage of homeland defense.

Among the weaknesses of the American colonists was that they were poorly organized, and the Continental Congress debated endlessly and took little action. A written constitution was not adopted until 1781 (The Articles of Confederation). The colonies were jealous of each other, there were currency problems, and taxation was nearly impossible. The American colonies suffered from a high inflation rate, and desertions from the army were common. The Continental Army had antiquated and inadequate firearms and not enough gunpowder. Clothing and uniforms were scarce; nearly 3000 Valley Forge soldiers went barefoot in the winter. Not surprisingly, the American soldiers were unreliable, and war profiteers weakened morale.

Figure 4.2: General La Fayette

American Secession

After the initial turmoil of the Boston Massacre, tensions eased between England and the colonies as the colonial economy improved. Then, in 1773, Parliament passed the Regulating and Tea Acts. England nationalized the struggling East India Company and began to export more tea to the American colonies at reduced prices. American merchants resisted because of the East India Company's monopoly. The sentiment of resistance spread based on the principle that American colonists did not want Parliament to tax the colonies. In December 1773, the Boston Sons of Liberty, led by Samuel Adams and John Hancock, organized a group dressed as Mohawk Indians to board three British ships filled with chests of tea. This became known as the Boston Tea Party. They dumped the tea overboard, and other groups in New York, Philadelphia, and Charleston also had tea parties in 1774.

Incensed, the English response was swift and harsh as the Parliament passed four acts known as the Coercive Acts by the British and the Intolerable Acts by the American colonists. The British shut down Boston Harbor and cut off trade, took over direct control of the Massachusetts government, allowed British officials accused of a crime to be tried only in England, and allowed British troops to be quartered in any colonial home. The King and his advisors considered the American colonies in open rebellion. They did not anticipate that other colonies would want to help Massachusetts. If Parliament could dissolve the Massachusetts government, American colonists in other colonies feared the same could happen to them. This led to the First Continental Congress in 1774.

Figure 4.3: The Boston Tea Party

When they met on September 5, 1774, the more radical delegates wanted active resistance to England, whereas moderates wanted conciliation. Most delegates to the First Continental Congress promised obedience to the King but denied Parliament's right to tax the colonies. The delegates set up an association to ban imports from England and exports to England. Estimates were that 20% of the colonists were loyal to Great Britain, 40% were active patriots, and 20% were on the fence. The delegates from every colony but Georgia issued a Declaration of Rights and Grievances: colonists retained the same rights as British subjects, including the right to elect representatives who would decide taxation and the right of trial by jury. The most important document from the First Continental Congress was the Continental Association.

The Association blamed the British Ministry for their miserable situation and recommended that a committee, mostly of ordinary colonists, be set up in every town, city, and county. These Committees of Inspection would take care of their communities and report on persons who violated the spirit of the Association. They also agreed to nonimportation, nonconsumption, nonexportation, and discontinuation of the slave trade. The purpose of the Association was to unite and manage the twelve revolutionary governments, set economic and moral policies, and empower the colonists. As noted, not all colonists agreed with the revolutionaries. Twenty percent were loyal to the crown, and 20% were undecided. Wealthy merchants, Anglican clergy, and colonists holding royal appointments were not party to the revolutionary agreements.

During the Second Continental Congress of May 1775, the delegates created a Continental Army and picked General George Washington as their commander. War had already broken out in Massachusetts. On April 19, 1775, the British military was ordered to seize the American militias' firearms and gunpowder stored at Lexington and Concord. The militia met the British regiment in Lexington, and someone fired, and the British fired back. The battle spread to Concord, and news of the conflict spread rapidly. Militia members, known as minutemen, assembled and drove the British back to Boston. The Minutemen gathered their numbers to over 20,000 and overtook the British in Boston. The colonial militia erected a fortification on Breed's Hill (which was misnamed Bunker Hill) overlooking the city. The British eventually got the colonial forces off the hill, but they suffered heavy casualties in so doing.

While the Minutemen and the British skirmished, the Continental Congress struggled to reach a consensus. Radicals, including John Adams, Samuel Adams, and John Hancock, begged the Congress to support Massachusetts. The Middle Colonies were more moderate, still calling for reconciliation with England. The South had radicals like Thomas Jefferson and Richard Henry Lee from Virginia and moderates like John and Edward Rutledge from South Carolina. The moderates feared that supporting the Minutemen would be a declaration of war against England. They finally compromised and formed the Continental Army with George Washington as commander in chief. At the same time, they attempted one more time to reconcile with the British.

Momentum began to point toward independence in 1776. A small pamphlet written by Thomas Paine began to circulate, *Common Sense*. Paine's pamphlet called for independence and denounced the monarchy, thereby capturing the spirit and imagination of the colonists. George Washington took control of the army and forced the British to retreat to Halifax. The royal governor of Virginia offered a proclamation that ensured the freedom of all indentured servants and slaves if they joined the British cause. Although the British motives were political and practical and not humanitarian, it was the first emancipation of enslaved people in American history. The British position brought more moderate Southerners into the revolutionary camp.

On June 7, 1776, Richard Henry Lee began the resolution process for independence. Congress passed it, but a separate committee had been assigned to draft a public declaration. Thomas Jefferson drafted the document, with John Adams and Benjamin Franklin edits. The famous preamble was genuinely revolutionary, relying upon natural law.

> We hold these truths to be self-evident, that all men are created equal, that they are endowed by their Creator with certain unalienable Rights, that among these are Life, Liberty and the pursuit of Happiness. That to secure these rights, Governments are instituted among Men, deriving their just powers from the consent of the governed, That whenever any Form of Government becomes destructive of these ends, it is the Right of the People to alter or to abolish it, and to institute new Government.

Congress approved the document on July 4, 1776. Clearly, declaring independence would not come without a steep price.

The War for Independence

The war began with the Battles of Lexington and Concord in 1775. It was a propaganda victory for the Americans, where 95 colonists were killed, and 270 British soldiers fell. This propelled the colonists into a more significant conflict with Great Britain, involving all the colonies, not just Massachusetts. With Congress declaring independence, there was no turning back, and the colonies now would face the full force of the world's most powerful military. The British abandoned Boston and assembled the largest expeditionary force in their history in New York. The force included tens of thousands of German mercenaries called Hessians. The hope was to cut off New England from the remaining colonies by seizing control of the Hudson River. New York was also home to many loyalists. In October 1776, the British attacked Brooklyn and Manhattan, forcing the Continental Army to retreat to New Jersey.

With the winter of 1776 approaching, General Washington needed a victory to boost the morale of his troops and the rest of the colonists. On Christmas Day, he led a surprise attack on the Hessian camp at Trenton by ferrying a few thousand colonial soldiers across the Delaware River at night. The daring attack was successful, and the Continental Army gained supplies and the psychological lift it needed to continue the war.

Figure 4.4: Washington Crossing the Delaware

In 1777, the Continental Army was victorious at Saratoga, New York, after the British invaded New York from Canada under General John Burgoyne. General William Howe abandoned Burgoyne and planned to attack Philadelphia instead. This strategic blunder led to Burgoyne's defeat at Saratoga and was a turning point in the war. Benjamin Franklin had been in France seeking an alliance, but the French were reluctant because they thought the Americans did not stand a chance against the British Empire. The Continental Army's victory at Saratoga convinced them otherwise. Franklin secured the alliance treaty with France on February 6, 1778. A colonial rebellion had turned into a global war between Great Britain and France.

Even though British General Howe had taken Philadelphia, he soon realized European-style fighting was for naught in North America. Controlling large cities did not strengthen the British hold on the colonies. General Washington realized he could not take the British forces head-on, so he favored small, frequent skirmishes and avoided large-scale battles. We would today call these guerilla tactics. In 1778, the British turned their attention to the South, assuming they would find more popular support. They captured cities once again but could not control the countryside. The Southern colonists fought among themselves, turning the Southern campaign into somewhat of a civil war.

The British fought France, Spain, and the Netherlands in addition to their war against the American colonists. Public support for the North American war was waning in Britain. General Washington marched his troops from New York to Virginia to trap the British southern army under the command of General Charles Cornwallis at Yorktown. With the support of the French Navy, the Continental and

French armies encircled Cornwallis, and he was forced to surrender the British forces. With a global war taking more of their attention and after failures in North America, England decided to call it quits, and peace negotiations began in France. The formal treaty was signed on September 3, 1783.

American colonists paid a heavy price for victory over the British—brutal winters, meager rations, and inadequate resources. Over 2500 American troops died at Valley Forge in the winter of 1777-1778. The war was hard on women and children as well. The British recruited American slaves, and estimates are that more than 30,000 formerly enslaved people joined the war. General Washington was initially reluctant to recruit former slaves but eventually relented. As hard as the war was on the colonists, the next period of forging a new nation would be even more difficult.

Assessment: Luck and Pluck (or Why the Rebels Won)

My friend, retired US Army Colonel Bill Wenger, authored a fascinating book on why the American colonies were able to beat the British (*The Key to American Independence: Quantifying Foreign Assistance to the American Revolution*). He provided a detailed analysis of the American victory in the American Revolutionary War, 1775–1783. The reasons include underestimating the colonial military, logistical complexities, bungled diplomacy, rugged American terrain (the British relied on ships while the Americans used crude roads), unconventional guerrilla tactics by the Americans, and the fact that the American Revolution was part of a wider world war. Most importantly, the bottom line was that the colonists could not have won without the help of France.

The Revolutionary Character of the American Revolution

In a political revolution, there is a sudden change in leaders and government. In a social revolution, there is a permanent alteration of society's social, economic, and ideological framework. Political revolutions can be short-lived, whereas social revolutions are longer-lasting. In assessing the character of the American Revolution, we need to ask if it created a permanent and substantial social, economic, and ideological change in the lives of most people in society. Although loyalist estates were confiscated and sold by the colonial legislatures, they were re-sold primarily to wealthy land speculators and varied by each colony (North Carolina being the exception). In other words, there was no real redistribution of wealth. Wealthy loyalists held most of the property and wealth in America before the revolution, and wealthy former loyalists held most of the property and wealth after the revolution. Slavery and indentures were abolished in the North but not in the South. With the British authority gone, new land out west was opened for settlement. Still, wealthy landowners tended to dominate the land rush, not small family landowners and former soldiers, who were not given the property they were promised at the outset of the war.

The colonial economic system was boosted by the victory over England. British debts were canceled, and American manufacturing grew and multiplied because the war cut off access to British goods. No longer under British restrictions, Americans were free to trade with whomever they wished. The Americans established their banks and a totally independent financial system. The American laissez-faire system was more independent than the British mercantilist system.

The Great Awakening had led people away from strict church doctrine and dogma. The leaders of the Revolution (who were part of the Enlightenment) believed in a natural rights philosophy. To bring everyone together, the patriots made a deal with the new and old light ministers (those ministers who practiced the new ways and those who adhered to the old ways): they would preserve religious freedom and the separation of church and state. Unfortunately, the secularization of the nation led to an anti-intellectual and emotional religion that was fearful of political power.

African Americans during the Revolution were swayed by the British, who offered freedom in exchange for service in the British military as the British courts abolished slavery in Great Britain. With a shortage of White volunteers, the colonial militias enlisted Black soldiers, which changed the way many viewed Black people. Many of the patriots called for the abolition of slavery in the colonies, making it illegal in New England and the Middle Colonies but not the Southern Colonies.

Women contributed to the Revolution through charities, fundraising, nursing, and other support roles. The first American women's associations were formed. At first, the efforts of women in the Revolution were applauded, but later, they were downplayed as "Martha Washington's Sewing Society." Ultimately, the Revolution produced no fundamental changes for women other than forming women's groups.

The Revolution tended to deemphasize sectional differences, which led to a tacit acceptance of slavery in the South. Myths surrounding the Founding Fathers, especially George Washington, emerged (i.e., telling the truth about chopping down a cherry tree, throwing a silver dollar across the Potomac River, and having wooden teeth). After the Revolution, there was an anti-colonial mentality and a distaste for imperialism. American society was strongly influenced by political, religious, and economic individualism. And the victory over the British gave Americans a sense of invincibility and a holy purpose. Lastly, the Puritan ethic was essential for success and would continue to influence domestic and foreign policy.

Conclusion

The American Revolution freed American colonists from British rule and spawned the age of democratic revolutions that spread to France, Haiti, and South

America. It also caused changes in England and its concept of empire, with British historians calling the period after the American Revolution the Second British Empire. The Americans now had the task of forming a new nation-state, the United States of America, but how exactly that nation would take shape and look was unclear. The first attempt at creating a lasting nation-state was with the Articles of Confederation in 1781 and eventually with the Constitution ratified in 1788. Historians have debated the causes and the character of the American Revolution. Was the Revolution caused by British imperial overreach or internal turmoil within the colonies? Were American colonists motivated primarily by constitutional convictions and principles, the concept of equality, or by economic self-interest? Was the American Revolution a true revolution? Was it radical or conservative? Invoking the words of the preamble to the Declaration of Independence is still driving debate in American politics today. How one frames the Revolution is fundamental to what it means to be American, the very heart of this book. A handful of Founding Fathers did not win the Revolution. Everyone participated: men and women, White and Black, rich and poor. But it did not totally live up to its high-minded ideals.

So, just how revolutionary was the American Revolution? It was more than just a political turnover or coup that replaced the British with American authority. It transformed America into a commercial nation with ambitions of global power, but there was no real redistribution of wealth. The rich remained wealthy, and the poor stayed poor. There was a religious transformation to adapt to secularism. Still, Americans were united under a Puritan moral ethic, impacting foreign relations and, because they failed to abolish slavery, had an uncertain attitude and false foundation for race relations. In sum, there were permanent changes, but it was still a very conservative revolution, and America has been very anti-revolutionary ever since.

Dear reader, with your indulgence, I would like to share a personal story involving a student of mine and the historical figure Patrick Henry that I think you will enjoy and find instructive.

It all started rather innocently. In 2003, I was awarded a Fulbright Teaching and Research Award. I was proud to be one of only 600 educators selected that year to travel abroad and teach my designated subject. My country was Norway, and my host institution was the University of Tromsø in Northern Norway. I was a natural selection for the Fulbright Committee because I spoke Norwegian and had traveled to Norway extensively. Accompanying me were my wife and my two young children.

When we arrived in Tromsø in 2003, I was immediately taken aback by the presence of Russian ships in the harbor. It made me nervous because I had served for six years in the US Army, learning to hate the Russians and consider them our enemies. I visited the university and was introduced to the staff and shown to my office (a large open room with a huge window facing the courtyard). I had seen this office in 1995 when I visited the university, and I had predicted I would one day work there. The office manager told me that my teaching schedule would be two classes, one with five graduate students and the other with 20 undergraduates. My Norwegian colleagues said that two classes constituted a heavy load. I could only laugh since I regularly have seven classes and over 300 students per semester at Citrus College, where I teach. We stayed with our Canadian friend and her family until the university found us a lovely two-bedroom, two-story condo.

After a few days of getting oriented to our new residence and the city, I was introduced to my teaching assistant (TA), also the wife of one of the professors. They were American expatriates. I got a weird feeling about them; my intuition was kicking in. Not long after the semester began, I heard stories from my graduate students about how these American expatriates were plotting behind my back. They thought I threatened them since they were vying for a permanent position at the university. My TA secretly passed on my instructional materials to her husband, who passed them on to a friend in the administration. She also told stories about my being late or not doing what I was supposed to do in the classroom.

We then had a Fulbright orientation in Oslo, the capital city. It was there that I first met the US Embassy personnel. One was the head of the Political and Economic Section, and the other was a Norwegian national who served as his executive assistant. My immediate impression of the assistant was that he was a CIA agent. His demeanor was somewhat gruff, and he had a swagger—not typical for most Norwegians. His first appearance was when the Political Section Chief was briefing us. He dropped a large box of booklets on the table behind us with a resounding crash. Everyone was startled, and he smiled in delight.

The Political Section Chief mentioned that he wanted to work with us in our capacities as academic ambassadors. I contacted the embassy several weeks later and spoke to him. He suggested a program called American Corners. I was asked to try to get it set up in Tromsø. One of my Norwegian colleagues informed me that the US government had previously maintained a secret CIA station in Tromsø, but it was shut down when the Norwegians discovered what was happening. The United States has had no intelligence-gathering operation in Tromsø since that time. The Political Section Chief asked me to talk to folks at the university to see if the American Embassy could donate materials to the library and designate part of an area for American cultural studies. The Norwegians immediately met this with skepticism. Later, I was put in contact with his assistant, the Norwegian National, whom I suspected of being a CIA agent. He was blunter than his boss and impressed upon me the importance of establishing this toehold to combat rabid anti-Americanism due to the Bush administration's foreign policies and the War in Iraq. Although it was becoming more evident what they wanted me to do, I wasn't ready to jump to conclusions.

Then, the embassy assistant asked if he could send two embassy officials to Tromsø to meet with faculty and students. I agreed and set up a forum for discussion of US foreign policy. I was to serve as the host for the two officers. We had a very lively meeting that was well attended. The young officers had their hands full with questions about the validity of the Bush Doctrine. Afterward, I invited them to lunch, but they declined because they had to return to Oslo. They asked me about my colleagues; they already knew their names, their political leanings (they were communists), and more than they should have known. They also knew the two American expatriates who had become my enemies. They impressed upon me the importance of establishing the American Corners.

I also got to teach some extraordinary young people, including a Russian student whose family lived in Tromsø. They were theatre people. His name was Sergei. He wanted to learn everything about America. One day, he walked up to me with immense pride.

"See what my mother has sewn on my jacket?" he said. I saw an American flag on the shoulder of his Levi's jean jacket. I was very moved. He always volunteered and spoke up in discussions. When we were to read Patrick Henry's "Give Me Liberty or Give Me Death" speech from the Second Virginia Convention in 1775 in the run-up to the American Revolution, Sergei volunteered and did a dramatic reading with great emotion. We all applauded. When I had to leave after the semester, the students gave me a going away party. They even invited the professor and his wife, who were trying to get rid of me—typical Norwegian diplomacy and peacemaking. A Norwegian student foolishly challenged Sergei to a vodka-drinking competition. After the festivities were over, I gave Sergei a present. It was an old baseball glove I had used in the 1980s. It was worn and faded, but he held it like a priceless heirloom. He told me he would cherish it forever.

We did not stay the whole academic year, as fate would have it. The family renting our home in Glendora, California, was late with the rent and threatened not to pay. We had no money saved, so we would miss our mortgage payment if they didn't pay their rent. We were working on very narrow financial margins. I had to decide to return to the United States early. The American expatriates were glad to be rid of me. I never got the toehold the embassy wanted in Tromsø before we left.

Russia is continually active in Northern Norway. The strategic importance of Norway's coastline was clear to the Germans, who invaded and occupied Norway during World War II. They wanted to control the shipping lanes to the Russian Kola

> Peninsula and the iron ore supply from Sweden through Narvik in Northern Norway. The Russians understand the continuing strategic importance of Northern Norway.
>
> Later, I discovered that American Corners was a CIA-sponsored project. The CIA was interested in Tromsø because of the many Russians in the city. American Corners was an attempt to establish a front for the CIA to spy on the Russians who were spying on the Norwegians in Northern Norway. Apparently, in trying to get me to establish American Corners, I almost became the CIA's unwitting operative. My intuition was correct about the CIA connection to the US Embassy and my fellow American academics, but I was wrong about the everyday Russian people. They are not our enemies. Part of my Cold War heart had melted due to Sergei's kindness and his love of the United States. Liberty is not just an American value.

Going back to two of the heroes of the beginning of the Revolution, Patrick Henry, and Thomas Paine, we can see what happens to true revolutionaries after the revolution has been won. After the American Revolution, Patrick Henry continued to play a significant role in shaping the young United States. Henry became a leader for the Anti-Federalists in Virginia. He opposed the Constitution's ratification because he believed it gave too much power to the national government. This opposition led to the first ten amendments to the Constitution, the Bill of Rights, a compromise allowing the southern states to ratify the document. Later, however, Henry supported John Adams, a Federalist, because he feared the unrest and radicalism that came with the French Revolution.

Thomas Paine saw the American Revolution as the beginning of a worldwide revolution for the average person's rights. In the 1790s, after the ratification of the Constitution, Paine moved to France and became deeply involved with the French Revolution. In 1791, he wrote *Rights of Man*, which defended the French Revolution against the criticism that the French had gone too far. Paine was convicted in absentia in England for the crime of seditious libel after he attacked conservative writer Edmund Burke.

It's fascinating how these two influential figures took divergent paths after the Revolution, each contributing to shaping the United States and dealing with revolution worldwide. In America, it was clear that the emphasis was on stability, not revolution. The excesses of the French Revolution may have frightened the Founding Fathers and contributed to the anti-revolutionary mindset in America. Despite that, fiery vestiges of revolution still exist in our society today. Take, for instance, the Latin phrase *sic semper tyrannis* that we encountered earlier in the chapter (which means thus be it to tyrants). That is what Brutus said to Julius Caesar when he and other Roman senators killed their emperor. It is what John Wilkes Booth said after he shot Abraham Lincoln. It is what was written on Timothy McVeigh's tshirt when they captured him after bombing the federal building in Oklahoma City in 1995. And it is also the state motto for Virginia—something to think about, for sure.

Recommended Sources

David McCullough. *1776: The Illustrated Edition.*

William V. Wenger. *The Key to American Independence: Quantifying Foreign Assistance to the American Revolution.*

Timeline of the Revolution. https://www.nps.gov/subjects/americanrevolution/timeline.htm.

Credits

Figure 4.1: John Adams. Source: https://commons.wikimedia.org/wiki/File:John_Adams_B%26W_(Biographical_Dictionary_of_America,_vol._1).png

Figure 4.2: General La Fayette. Source: https://commons.wikimedia.org/wiki/File:Gilbert_du_Motier_Marquis_de_Lafayette.jpg

Figure 4.3: The Boston Tea Party. Source: https://springfieldmuseums.org/collections/item/the-destruction-of-tea-at-boston-harbor-nathaniel-currier/

Figure 4.4: Washington Crossing the Delaware. Source: https://commons.wikimedia.org/wiki/File:Washington_Crossing_the_Delaware_by_Emanuel_Leutze,_MMA-NYC,_1851.jpg

CHAPTER FIVE

Founding America

> Objectives
> 1. Understand the significance of the Bill of Rights.
> 2. Identify the arguments presented by both the Federalists and the Anti-Federalists.
> 3. Compare the experiences of the Native Americans and African Americans.
> 4. Comprehend the significance and legacy of the War of 1812.

The American Revolution had both short- and long-term consequences. Once the Declaration of Independence was signed, each state had to create its constitution based on popular sovereignty. The Revolution unleashed forces of change in terms of politics, social structure, and the economy. The most significant changes were the increased participation in politics and government by regular people, the concept of religious toleration, and a focus on continuing growth, especially westward. Expansion west meant more conflicts with Native Americans who were being pushed off their ancestral lands. The Articles of Confederation made the postwar Congress weak and ineffective. Political and social life changed after the Revolution as more people gained the right to vote and took on local government positions. American society was less aristocratic and more egalitarian. The most significant long-term change was the end of the British mercantilist economy. Domestic markets and manufacturing took off and drove the push westward.

Not much changed for women in postwar America, despite the support role women played in the Revolution. Many loyalists, who had supported England during the Revolutionary War, left America and lived in exile (up to 60,000 people). Some lived in England but were strangers in the land they supported. Others ended up in Newfoundland, New Brunswick, and Quebec. The Treaty of Paris had a provision to protect the property of loyalists, but most lost everything as the Americans did not honor that agreement. Thousands of formerly enslaved loyalists who fought with the British hoped that England would uphold their promise of freedom and help them establish homes elsewhere in the British Empire. Many ended up in Canada and some settled in Sierra Leone in Africa. They continued to face social and economic hardships and marginalization.

Some Americans were inspired by their fight for liberty from the British and freed their slaves. Most northern states passed emancipation laws. However, in the lower South, many former slaves were forced back into bondage. The rhetoric of "all men are created equal" fell silent, and in the long term, the Revolution failed to reconcile slavery with the concept of liberty for all. Eventually, this would boil over in the mid-1800s, leading to the American Civil War. The support that Native Americans gave to the British was a pretense to justify expansion westward and moving Native tribes from their land. Sadly, the gaining of American independence signaled the end of what was left of Native American independence.

Articles of Confederation and the Constitution

Richard Henry Lee proposed a formal plan for union among the colonies in 1777. A year later, the Articles of Confederation were adopted by Congress, although not ratified by the states until 1781. In 1783, Congress was threatened by angry Revolutionary War veterans demanding what they were promised, including pay and land. Congress moved to Princeton, New Jersey, and a year later moved again to New York until the new capital was selected. The Articles of Confederation would not work for the new nation. Congress lacked the power over commerce, and the new government could not make agreements with foreign countries because individual states could veto any treaty. In 1786, the Virginia House of Burgesses passed a statute written by Thomas Jefferson, supported by James Madison, which addressed religious freedom. That statute helped form the first amendment to the Constitution.

At the 1786 Annapolis Convention (September 11–14), the delegates hoped to address the economic challenges faced by the independent states. Of particular concern was the regulation of interstate commerce. Unfortunately, only five states (Delaware, New Jersey, New York, Pennsylvania, and Virginia) bothered to send delegates. With limited representation at the convention, progress on the pressing issues was almost impossible. Alexander Hamilton, who was in favor of a strong central government (a Federalist), proposed that another convention be held the following year to address broader issues—the eventual Constitutional Convention in Philadelphia in 1787 could not come soon enough because it seemed as though the United States were (using the plural tense intentionally because that is how it was written until after the Civil War) not so united.

Shays' Rebellion

Conflict usually emerges from weakness. The Articles of Confederation were not a strong enough bond for the new country. Shays' Rebellion was a significant radical uprising that highlighted this weakness. The rebellion began in 1786 in western Massachusetts. The post-war economy was messy due to runaway inflation and heavy taxes levied to pay off the Revolutionary War debts. The farmers, many of whom were veterans, were in trouble because they could not pay their taxes or debts. They faced the loss of their property and even imprisonment. Daniel Shays, a captain in the Continental Army, led the rebellion as he and others took up arms against what they considered an oppressive government. Their attack targeted any symbol of authority, such as courthouses. The rebellion ended at the federal Springfield Armory in early 1787. Shays and others were condemned to death by the Supreme Court of Massachusetts, but Shays was later pardoned. The rebellion reminded those in government that a strong constitution was needed.

Figures 5.1 and 5.2: Daniel Shays and Shays' Forces Flee Continental Troops

The Constitutional Convention

The Constitutional Convention began on May 25, 1787. The delegates planned to work together to create a successful government framework for the newly independent states. They needed to address issues such as representation, federalism, commerce, and individual rights. Every state except Rhode Island attended the convention. One of the first orders of business was to name a convention president.

George Washington returned to private life after the Revolutionary War but always advocated for a strong union and was a leading Federalist. He called the Articles of Confederation "a rope of sand" and feared the country was headed for anarchy and needed a robust national constitution. Benjamin Franklin nominated George Washington to preside over the Constitutional Convention.

The mandated mission was to revise the Articles of Confederation and form a new government. Virginia had a plan. The Virginia Plan called for a new form of government with three branches: an executive, judiciary, and legislative (with two houses based on population). The opposing New Jersey Plan called for equal representation of states in a unicameral congress and modified the Articles of Confederation. The Connecticut Compromise proposed that the lower house be based on population and that the upper house should have equal representation. Based on the compromise, a rough draft of the constitution was made. The drafting process of the US Constitution is often referred to as the framing and the delegates as the framers. Two of the most challenging issues to deal with were proportional representation and slavery, and they were tied together. The northern states, where slavery was already in the process of abolition, disagreed with the southern states, whose agricultural economies relied on slavery. Unfortunately, the delegates agreed to protect slavery as an institution and would count each slave as three-fifths of a person for proportional representation. They also agreed to return escaped slaves to their owners. The Constitution was approved on September 17, 1787, but still had to be ratified by each state.

The Northwest Ordinance

The Northwest Ordinance, also known as the Ordinance of 1787, was enacted by the Congress on July 13, 1787. It established the Northwest Territory, encompassing land beyond the Appalachian Mountains, between British North America and the Great Lakes north and the Ohio River south. The western boundary was the Mississippi River. The ordinance established the sovereignty of the federal government and stated that westward expansion would be through the admission of new states and not the expansion of existing states. Slavery was prohibited in the new territory, establishing a geographical divide between slave and free states, an extension of the Mason-Dixon line. The Mason-Dixon line is a demarcation line that separated four states (Pennsylvania, Maryland, Delaware, and West Virginia). The line along the southern border of Pennsylvania became known as the boundary between the slave and free states.

The Federalist Papers

John Jay, James Madison, and Alexander Hamilton wrote the Federalist Papers. The 85 essays defended the new constitution as it was going through ratification. During that time, there was a fierce battle between Federalists and Anti-Federalists, whose echoes are still heard today. In addition to Hamilton, Madison, and Jay, George Washington was also a Federalist. They were all disillusioned by the weakness of the Articles of Confederation, which caused economic and political instability. They believed that a strong federal government that could levy taxes, regulate commerce, and enforce and interpret laws was essential for the United States to survive.

The Anti-Federalists, including Patrick Henry, George Mason, and Thomas Jefferson, feared that a strong central government would undermine individual liberty and states' rights. They insisted on a Bill of Rights protecting citizens against political tyranny. They preferred that power resides with the state and local governments.

Ultimately, the two sides compromised by including the first ten constitutional amendments in the ratification process. The disagreements were more profound than surface opinions; they struck at the heart of American governance and the balance between centralized power and individual rights. The argument originated in Greek philosophy, where Plato posited that man could not live without freedom or authority. The key is striking the right balance, something we still argue about today in America.

Ratifying the Constitution

The five-member Committee of Style (Hamilton, Madison, William Samuel Johnson, Rufus King, and Gouverneur Morris) drafted the last version of the 4200-word Constitution. On September 17, 1787, George Washington was the first to sign the document. Not all the Constitutional Convention delegates signed. Thirty-nine of the 55 members signed. It was then time to send it to the states for ratification. Nine of the 13 states would have to ratify the Constitution for it to go into effect. Gouverneur Morris is one of the lesser-known signers of the document, but it was Morris who tightened up the language, especially the beginning of the famous preamble.

On December 7, 1787, five states (Delaware, Pennsylvania, New Jersey, Georgia, and Connecticut) ratified the Constitution. Massachusetts, among other states, opposed the document. They noted that it failed to reserve undelegated powers to the states and lacked constitutional protection for political rights such as freedom of speech, freedom of religion, and freedom of the press. In February 1788, Massachusetts and other holdout states reached a compromise with the Federalists based on assurances that amendments would be proposed to address their concerns. Massachusetts, Maryland, and South Carolina were then on board, along with New Hampshire. With enough states ratifying the Constitution, it was agreed that the government under the US Constitution would begin on March 4, 1789. George Washington was inaugurated as the first US president on April 30, 1789. Rhode Island was the last of the 13 states to ratify the Constitution.

Figure 5.3: President George Washington

The Bill of Rights

The compromise that got the reluctant states to ratify was the first 10 amendments to the Constitution. James Madison, as a congressman, introduced 19 amendments, of which only 10 were ratified by the states, and became part of the Constitution on December 10, 1791. Collectively known as the Bill of Rights, those 10 amendments guarantee freedom of speech, religion, the press, the right to bear and keep arms, the right to assemble peaceably, protection from unreasonable search and seizure, and the right to a speedy and public trial by an impartial jury. Madison became known as the Father of the Constitution based on his work in drafting the document and helping in its ratification.

Even though James Madison drafted the Bill of Rights, he believed the Constitution was acceptable without including the amendments. He was concerned that being too specific in spelling out individual rights could eventually be limiting. There have been thousands of proposed amendments since the Constitution was ratified, but only 17 have been added since the original 10. It is an arduous process where three-quarters of the states must approve any new amendment. In the two centuries since the Constitution was ratified, America has grown in territory and power, probably more so than the framers had envisioned. They knew it was not a perfect document, which is why the amendment process is embedded. At the closing of the Constitutional Convention in 1787, Benjamin Franklin said:

"I agree to this Constitution with all its faults, if they are such, because I think a central government is necessary for us… I doubt too whether any other Convention we can obtain may be able to make a better Constitution."

Figure 5.4: President James Madison

Winston Churchill, the wartime Prime Minister of England during World War Two, said:

"Many forms of Government have been tried and will be tried in this world of sin and woe. No one pretends that democracy is perfect or all-wise. Indeed, it has been said that democracy is the worst form of Government except for all those other forms that have been tried from time to time."

My take on forming the Constitution is that democracy is messy, fraught with peril, confusion, frustration, and uncertainty, but there is no better alternative to democracy. Try living in an ant colony if you want certainty and absolute order.

Compromise

Although debates about the power of the federal government continued during Washington's two terms in office, his election gave the Constitution undisputed authority. Much of the sting of anti-federalism went away when the Bill of Rights was ratified by 1791. James Madison supported the amendments as a compromise and against his wishes. As necessary as they were, they did not provide any voice for women, voting was still restricted to those with property, and slavery continued to exist. New England and the Deep South had made an agreement that protected the foreign slave trade for 20 years in exchange for making it easier for Congress to pass commercial legislation. Consequently, the Atlantic slave trade continued until 1808, when it was outlawed by Great Britain, after a slave revolt in Haiti, and the end of France's expansion in North America and subsequent sale of the Louisiana Territory at a bargain price. The so-called Louisiana Purchase of 1803 doubled the size of the United States and led many to believe that slavery would slowly go away as the country expanded westward.

Alexander Hamilton

President George Washington had a remarkably dynamic cabinet. His vice president was John Adams, Alexander Hamilton was his treasury secretary, and Thomas Jefferson was his secretary of state. Three of them were Federalists, and Jefferson was an Anti-Federalist. Washington struggled to reconcile the factions within his administration. Hamilton believed that self-interest is what drove all human actions. That need to accumulate property and wealth is what drove commerce and industry. He thought the government needed to protect private property and steer human desire toward the public good. Hamilton did not believe in an equal distribution of property. His concept was to protect the rights of the wealthy, harness their wealth, and drive for the betterment of the government and, thereby, the nation.

Alexander Hamilton's plan involved assuming the state debts from the Revolutionary War (about $25 million) and creating a Bank of the United States. He wanted to link federal government power and the financial strength of the economy. Creditors who owned state bonds would receive new federal notes of the same value. Hamilton believed these notes would circulate like money and spur the economy, but there were objections. Taxpayers would be paying face value on original notes that had lost value, and most of the original notes had been sold to speculators at a cheap price. That meant that the government would be rewarding speculators with a windfall profit. The southern states had already paid their debts, so they felt Hamilton's plan meant they had to pay for part of New England's debt. President

Washington and Congress approved Hamilton's plan against the objections based on the thought that all government debt needed to be paid in full; otherwise, people would lose trust in the government.

Figure 5.5: Alexander Hamilton

Hamilton's Bank of the United States was also approved, but there was again opposition. Thomas Jefferson argued that the Constitution did not permit Congress to create a bank. Hamilton countered that it was constitutional, and a federal bank would act as a depository for federal funds and print paper banknotes backed by gold and silver. The Bank of the United States could also control inflation by taking back the bank notes and demanding gold and silver in exchange. The bank would also encourage wealthy investors to participate in the government's finances. In 1791, Congress approved a charter for the Bank of the United States, which helped create securities markets, allowed the federal government to borrow money, and supported the spread of state-chartered banks and private business corporations. However, for those on the frontier who lacked capital, Hamilton's plans seemed to reinforce economic class boundaries and allow wealthy people to control the federal government. More trouble came when Hamilton proposed a federal excise tax on producing, selling, and consuming goods like whiskey. As brilliant as Hamilton was, he should have seen this coming.

The Whiskey Rebellion

Most American farmers considered grain to be their most valuable crop. Western farmers preferred to sell grain to local distilleries for alcohol production because it was more profitable than shipping to the east coast over the Appalachians. Alexander Hamilton's whiskey tax was a heavy burden for Western farmers and distillers. Small producers argued that it disadvantaged them because they paid 9¢ per gallon compared to the 6¢ paid by larger producers. Additionally, only cash was accepted for tax payments. The whiskey tax divided the republic into east and west, merchants and farmers, and urban and rural. In 1791, farmers disguised as women tarred and feathered a tax collector in western Pennsylvania. Local sheriffs and deputies who tried to find the assailants had a similar fate. These rebel farmers used the same tactics in the Revolution and Shays' Rebellion. Refusals to pay the tax were common, and tax collectors encountered defiance and threats. Incidents escalated, including the tarring and feathering of more excise tax officers. The situation reached a breaking point. Tax collections dwindled as a result.

In July 1794, roving groups of rebel farmers attacked tax collectors and federal marshals and burnt down the homes of two tax officials. An armed force of 7000 led by attorney David Bradford robbed the US mail and assembled eight miles east of Pittsburgh. President Washington simultaneously sent a delegation to discuss a resolution and organized an army of 13,000 militiamen in Carlisle, Pennsylvania. On September 19, George Washington led his troops into a fight with the rebels. As Washington's army moved west, the rebels scattered. Alexander Hamilton was put in charge of trying the insurgents, most of whom were released, with two sentenced to death for treason. Washington pardoned those two men. The Whiskey Rebellion proved that the federal government could put down internal conflict, led to the rise of the Republican Party (overtaking the Federalist Party), and showed how distrustful poor citizens in the West were of the government.

Figure 5.6: Whiskey Rebellion

Jay Treaty

Alexander Hamilton was ambitious and determined to create a solid American financial system. He wanted the United States to be active in foreign trade and not isolated. To do this, America would have to establish a friendly relationship with Great Britain, which was not easy. England and America had a tense relationship made worse by the war between France and Great Britain. American sailors were impressed by the British Navy and forced to serve, which not only threatened free trade but also the civil liberties of American citizens. President Washington declared official neutrality in April 1793, and John Jay, the Chief Justice of the US Supreme Court, traveled to London to negotiate a treaty. There was significant opposition, especially from Jefferson and Madison, who believed the treaty favored England over France. Republicans thought that the French, who had overthrown their monarch in a revolution, would welcome a friendship with the United States and vice versa. Jefferson and Madison suspected that a treaty with England would favor northern merchants and manufacturers over the agricultural industry of the South.

John Jay signed a "treaty of amity, commerce, and navigation" with the British in November 1794. Jay's Treaty (the more common name for the document) required England to remove its military presence in the Northwest Territory (specifically Fort Detroit, Fort Mackinac, and Fort Niagara) by 1796. England also agreed to reimburse American merchants for losses, and the United States agreed to a most favored nation trade status with Great Britain. The treaty moved America onto England's side in their war with France, and it did not prevent the impressment of American sailors. Federalists heralded the treaty to position the United States as a neutral trading partner, thereby promoting prosperity and economic growth. However, for Jefferson and his Republicans, the treaty proved that the Federalists favored a monarchy over a republic and even allowed American citizens to be denied their liberty. The American political system was slowly being transformed into two opposing political parties.

The Impact of the French Revolution

Federalists saw the 1789 French Revolution (especially the beheading of the French monarchy) as radicalism that needed to be stopped. The United States had already had Shays' Rebellion, the Whiskey Rebellion, and other forms of agitation, and Federalists wanted to maintain order and stability above all. Although America was founded through revolution, a strain of anti-revolutionary thought persisted among the Federalists and continues to influence us today.

When French ambassador Citizen Edmond-Charles Genêt arrived in the United States in April 1793, he was greeted with great fanfare throughout the United States, but then the trouble began. He encouraged the United States to attack the Spanish colonies in Florida and Louisiana and began to appeal directly to the American people. President Washington had had enough and ordered the French ambassador out of the country. Genêt remained in the United States because back home in France, a radical coalition of French revolutionaries had seized control, and he feared for his life. As the guillotine was working overtime and the body count was mounting back in France, Americans began to have second thoughts about the French Revolution. Jefferson was steadfast in his support for the revolution, however.

There was a peaceful transfer of power after the 1796 election in the United States, calming the fears that the French Revolution would negatively impact America. Washington's vice president, John Adams, became the nation's second president. He faced the challenges of not being as popular as Washington and the chaos in Europe. France began to attack American shipping in response to Jay's Treaty. Adams sent diplomats to France in 1797 to resolve the crisis, but when it was revealed that only bribes could stimulate discussions with the French, Adams came under fire at home (the so-called XYZ Affair, named after the code names for the diplomats). Some Americans began clamoring for war with France. Many people expected the French Navy to arrive at any moment and attack America. Ironically, the same navy helped us win the American Revolutionary War. Southerners feared that the French would bring in Black troops to help liberate the American slaves in the South. There were also strong feelings of anger and fear toward France in New England.

A rumor started by Jedidiah Morse, a Massachusetts minister, proposed that the French Revolution was a conspiracy by an anti-Christian cabal known as the Illuminati. French naval ships engaged American merchant ships on the high seas, which led to the passage of the Alien and Sedition Acts in 1798. The intent was to expose French agents and fellow travelers from subverting American defenses. Unfortunately, they punished anyone who criticized the president and the Federalist Party, thereby threatening First Amendment rights. Federalists argued that speech that attacks the security or welfare of the government should not be protected. The American Revolution was much more conservative than many had imagined, and the ensuing debates on free speech seem to be echoed today. Some Americans felt they had the right to say almost anything without prosecution. Jefferson had initially argued for the Alien and Sedition Acts, saying that the United States should punish Americans who speak "false facts" that injured the country. Later, however, Jefferson and Madison felt that the states should declare such federal laws unconstitutional. These debates made Americans question just what the limits, if any, of liberty were. Was American liberty radical and free or was it more traditional and constrained like Great Britain?

Freedom of Religion

In addition to free speech guaranteed in the First Amendment, freedom of religion exists. At the end of the 1700s, a shift in American attitudes about religion was taking place. When signing the Declaration of Independence, no American colony practiced separation of church and state. All 13 states had tax-supported churches or required professions of a particular faith for officeholders. Many felt it was necessary to protect the social order and some semblance of morality in society. Disestablishment (separating the government from the church) started in all the states, with Massachusetts being the last to do so in 1833. In 1790, South Carolina removed its religious restrictions on politicians. Many states held that the religious freedom clause in the First Amendment was not considered applicable to state governments. Thomas Jefferson and James Madison favored disestablishment because they saw a connection between the church and state as a tool of oppression. America has a history of an uneasy separation of church and state. Most Supreme Court cases waiting to be considered today involve freedom of religion.

Election of 1800

President Adams was highly disappointed with the reaction of most Americans to his Alien and Sedition Acts. They had lost confidence in him, and in 1798 on Thanksgiving, angry rioters forced President Adams and his family out of Philadelphia, still the capital city. Even Alexander Hamilton gave him little support. The election of 1800 was particularly nasty, even by American standards today. A Federalist newspaper predicted that if a Republican won, America would be filled with chaos and criminality. Republican newspapers raised doubts about President

Adams' sexual orientation. Thomas Jefferson won the election only after dozens of votes by the House of Representatives (since no candidate had enough electoral votes). Republicans believed Jefferson's victory saved the United States from an aristocratic takeover.

Figure 5.7: Thomas Jefferson

Thomas Jefferson offered peace with the Federalists in his inaugural address. He wanted to secure the rights of the minority Federalist party. Many considered the Republican victory a bloodless revolution. Adams left the White House in a peaceful transition of power. Jefferson wanted to decrease the federal government's influence while the Supreme Court sought to strengthen its authority. The 1803 Marbury vs. Madison case was significant as it pitted the executive against the judiciary. On his way out of office, John Adams and Congress passed the Judiciary Act of 1801, which created new courts, added judges, and gave the president more control over appointing judges. Adams made several justices of peace appointments in Washington, DC (the so-called Midnight Appointments) before Jefferson took office. A judge named William Marbury was one of those appointed by Adams. When Jefferson took over, James Madison, the new secretary of state, refused

Marbury's commission. The Marbury case went up to the Supreme Court, where Chief Justice John Marshall delivered the opinion. Although Marbury was entitled to his commission, the Supreme Court could not grant it because Section 13 of the Judiciary Act of 1789 conflicted with Article III Section 2 of the US Constitution. Marshall ruled that the provision enabling Marbury to bring his claim to the Supreme Court was unconstitutional. This decision established the principle of judicial review, giving the American Supreme Court the power to strike down laws that violated the Constitution. Thus began a new era of what has been called Jeffersonian Democracy.

Jeffersonian Democracy

The victory of the Democratic-Republicans over the Federalists, led by Thomas Jefferson, was the beginning of changes to the republic. All Americans, wealthy, poor, Native Americans, enslaved Americans, and women sought a seat at the table of freedom and liberty. In Richmond, Virginia, in August 1800, a slave revolt began. It started with some diversionary fires. Then, an informant alerted Governor James Monroe, and the state militia was called in to stop the rebellion. The conspirators were captured, and the leader, an enslaved man named Gabriel, and 25 others were tried and executed. Virginia subsequently placed more restrictions on free Black people as a result. White American slaveholders knew that Haiti had a successful slave rebellion in 1793, and they feared what would happen in America. Although the Enlightenment inspired the Founding Fathers to create the United States under the blessings of liberty and freedom for all, political compromise caused the framers to fail to reach their lofty ideals and eliminate slavery. Every rationale was used to justify slavery, religion, culture, and race. Then, some claimed there were genetic differences between the races relating to intelligence and even postulated that Blacks were a distinct species of human. Thomas Jefferson subscribed to some of these absurd ideas. Some Americans feared that the races could not peacefully coexist and began supporting the repatriation of Black people back to Africa.

Many working people were excited about Jefferson's election because they felt he could restore more direct control for citizens over their government. Wealthy Americans were not silent about their disdain for handing political power to the masses. They believed that pure democracy would lead to anarchy. Jefferson thought that a government that answered directly to the people would strengthen the bonds of the national union and not create anarchy—free people governing themselves democratically, not the Federalist model of a powerful central government. Republicans emphasized the role of women in the Revolution and the formation of the nation. They believed that women could nurture the principles of liberty and teach their children the values of independence to ensure freedom for future generations of Americans.

Jefferson was one of the most intellectually gifted presidents we have had. President John F. Kennedy once said while dining with Nobel Prize winners in 1962:

"I think this is the most extraordinary collection of talent, of human knowledge, that has ever been gathered together at the White House, with the possible exception of when Thomas Jefferson dined alone." Jefferson was a politician, statesman, diplomat, intellectual, writer, scientist, and philosopher. He believed that government should be small, simple, and frugal. His concept of America was a peaceful nation of yeoman farmers. He once said, "Those who labor in the earth are the chosen people of God." As remarkable as he was, Jefferson was not without his faults. He carried on an affair with one of his slaves, Sally Hemings (now proven by DNA testing). Moreover, Jefferson believed that African Americans were inferior and never acknowledged that slavery was the basis for the agrarian success of the nation and was incompatible with the ideals of liberty that he espoused. He also never accounted for Native Americans or their rights in his plans for a grand republic. Thomas Jefferson is full of contradictions. On the one hand, he struggled and fought for the rights and opportunities of ordinary people. But, despite his eloquent words in the Declaration of Independence, "that all men are created equal," Jefferson not only owned slaves, but he also never set them free (unlike George Washington).

Lewis and Clark and the Corps of Discovery

The Lewis and Clark Expedition (also known as the Corps of Discovery) was an extraordinary journey and human accomplishment between May 1804 and September 1806. President Thomas Jefferson asked Meriwether Lewis to explore the lands west of the Mississippi River—the Louisiana Purchase that Jefferson had negotiated with France. Lewis chose William Clark as his co-leader for the mission. Lewis and Clark were tasked with exploring the lands of the Louisiana Purchase, finding a practical route across the continent, and establishing an American hold on the new territory. There are many lessons and morals to be drawn from the expedition of Lewis and Clark. They were looking for the Northwest Passage—a continuous navigable waterway between the Atlantic and Pacific oceans. The two explorers opened the West to further exploration and settlement and opened the West to the American imagination. Just think of how many Western movies and TV shows have been made. People worldwide, even if they do not know much else about America, have heard of cowboys, Indians, and the Wild West. Lewis and Clark helped invent an American national identity.

The expedition faced harsh weather, unforgiving terrain, treacherous waters, injuries, starvation, disease, and encounters with both friendly and hostile Native Americans, including a Native American woman named Sacajawea (from the Lemhi Shoshone Tribe), who saved them on several occasions. Despite being only a teenager, she served courageously as a translator and guide who had intimate knowledge of the terrain and Native peoples of the West. Sacajawea had been captured by a Hidatsa raiding party when she was only 12 years old and was later sold to a French-Canadian fur trapper. Their journey was considered a success, and Sacajawea's role was invaluable. Lewis and Clark collected valuable geographic, ecological, and cultural data about a previously uncharted area of North America.

Figure 5.8: Lewis and Clark with Sacajawea

Since the time of Lewis and Clark, every subsequent generation has viewed their expedition differently. Lewis and Clark saw themselves primarily as Army officers on a military mission, and their mission was clear: Secure the West and its wealth for the United States. America needed to claim its Louisiana Purchase territory before the Europeans did. Spain controlled the south and Great Britain the north. Being a scientist and a politician, Thomas Jefferson also charged the duo with expanding scientific knowledge and furnishing them with scientific instruments. Still, the expansion of US power was the chief goal. Guarding against a tendency toward presentism when studying the past, we must see the men of the Corps of Discovery as soldiers, not saints, and their commanders were realistic men of their time.

After 8000 miles and 28 months of travel from their start near St. Louis, the corps returned to a short-lived hero's welcome. President Jefferson was disappointed because his dream of a land with abundant water, conveniently tied to the Pacific Ocean, where self-sufficient farmers could live in a democratic Shangri-la far from Washington politics, corruption, and corrosive issues like slavery, did not come true. The story did not have a happy ending. The West, although beautiful and largely pristine, was a harsh and often inhospitable place with treacherous and foreboding mountain ranges and where peace with the Native Americans would only come by brute force and a series of broken treaties. To cap it all off, Lewis, who was a chronic depressive person, shot and killed himself in Tennessee in 1809 while on a trip to Washington to justify his expense report to a government bureaucrat.

The War of 1812

The War of 1812 is often referred to as the Second American Revolution. The Americans fought the British again, mainly because of how Americans were being mistreated. After the American Revolution, it was assumed the United States would be free from British interference at home. However, that was not the case. The British remained in the United States, supported the Native Americans in their conflicts with Americans, and had military forts strategically placed near the Great Lakes. The Napoleonic Wars were also a catalyst in the War of 1812. The fighting between France and England left the United States in the middle between the belligerent European powers and led to an infringement on American neutral shipping rights.

Native Americans had been fighting for their land since the arrival of the Europeans. In 1810, Tenskwatawa and Tecumseh met with Indiana Territorial Governor William Henry Harrison to resolve the problem of Americans "buying" land from them without their consent. However, instead of resolving the issue, the meeting turned into a battle that ended in a stalemate. From then on, the violence escalated, leaving many Americans believing that the British were supplying the Natives with weaponry and encouragement. Western farmers were incredibly unsettled and called for Congress to declare war on Great Britain.

The Napoleonic Wars began in 1803 between France and England. During the war, the British Navy controlled the seas. Napoleon Bonaparte ordered European nations such as Russia and Prussia to stop trading with the British. England retaliated by attempting a blockade of Europe. This British blockade hurt the American economy, especially the southern states as they were hardest hit. "The Orders in Council" was a proclamation that allowed British captains to seize crewmembers from foreign ships whom they considered British (this procedure was called impressment). Impressments of US sailors soon became a major reason for hostilities between England and the United States.

In 1807, a US frigate named The Chesapeake left for the Mediterranean. Not far from American territorial waters, a British ship called The Leopard stopped the Chesapeake and demanded the right to search it for British sailors. The US captain refused to let them aboard, so the Leopard fired on them. As a result, 18 Americans were killed, and outrage against England grew exponentially as the British attacked a passenger ship and killed innocent Americans.

If it were up to a majority opinion in America, the country would have gone to war with Britain immediately after the attack on The Chesapeake. However, President Thomas Jefferson decided to take a different approach: He pushed through the Embargo Act of 1807. The Embargo Act meant that no supplies would leave or enter any American port. He had hoped that this act would weaken the British economy. Not only did his plan backfire, but it was also remarkably ineffective. Many disobeyed the act and would conduct their trade out to sea and out of sight. In 1809, Congress repealed the Embargo Act.

James Madison became president in 1809, and with a new president came new congressmen determined to take a bolder stand against Great Britain. These latest members of Congress believed that British Canada should also be part of the United States. Their logic was that Canada was also part of the deal when the United States won its independence from England. Congressman Henry Clay was the leader of the War Hawks, who favored war with England and extended pressure on President Madison to declare war. The War Hawks were mostly younger members of Congress from the South and the West. Their agenda was the nation's expansion (by acquiring Canada and Florida and pushing further west through Native American resistance), and they figured that war with England would help them achieve that goal. The War Hawks eventually got what they wanted, with President Madison declaring war on June 18, 1812, following a narrow vote in Congress.

Even though war was not declared until late June 1812, the US government had been preparing for war. They had already asked for volunteers to bolster the relatively small US military. American forces commanded by General William Hull started marching from Ohio to Fort Detroit in late May with plans to invade Canada. Later that summer, Hull had to surrender Fort Detroit to the British forces—it was a disaster. American ships began attacking British naval vessels without the English captains knowing that war had been declared. One of the critical battles was at Fort Meigs in Perrysburg, Ohio. Dear reader, I want to share a personal story about that battle site.

It was Memorial Day weekend in the spring of 1990 when I took my two older sons (nine and 10 years old) to a War of 1812 battle reenactment at Ft. Meigs in Perrysburg, Ohio. It was a bright, sunny day, and the temperature was mild. The boys were excited to see all the soldiers in their period uniforms marching around the fort. There were encampments and music and demonstrations of how to fire a flintlock rifle—lots of smoke and noise. Of course, we saw the bad guys (the British) in their iconic red coats. We booed and hissed at them. How fun!

Fort Meigs was on the frontier of the Northwest Territory of the young United States. From June 1812 to February 1813, American forces had already lost fortifications at Fort Mackinac and Detroit in the Michigan Territory and Fort Dearborn in the Illinois Territory. They had also been defeated in a major battle at Raisin River in Michigan. From April 30 through May 9, 1813, over 1200 American soldiers under the command of General William Henry Harrison (who later became president of the United States) held Fort Meigs against British troops, Canadian troops, and their Native American allies. Over 600 Americans died in the battle, and some are still buried on the site. The American victory at Fort Meigs turned the tide of the war.

We were having so much fun watching the reenactment and seeing history unfold in front of our eyes. We imagined what it must have been like in those days when we were fighting in a war. I had been in the US Army and had fired many weapons and come close to going to war, but I was never in combat. I stressed to the boys the seriousness of war and how they should handle weapons carefully. We were watching an American cannon crew prepare for firing. They, of course, were not firing cannon balls since this was only a demonstration, not an actual war, but it was still loud and scary, and the boys had to cover their ears. As the cannon crew readied their shot, another soldier wandered carelessly in front of the cannon and did not hear or heed the warning of imminent firing. They lit the cannon's fuse with the careless soldier standing directly in front of the barrel. Boom! The blast threw him six feet into the air and forward from the concussion of the explosion coming from the business end of the cannon. His fellow soldiers came to his aid, and he was soon back on his feet, not seriously hurt but shaken up. It was quite an impressive, however unintentional, demonstration. I am glad the Americans prevailed in the battle; otherwise, I would be writing this story in British English. Cheerio!

Figure 5.9: Siege of Fort Meigs

Another famous battle at the war's end was in New Orleans, Louisiana, where a new American hero emerged who would later become president and change the American political system. Major General Andrew Jackson was tasked with defending New Orleans from British capture. In January 1815, they were preparing for the British advance. Not only did General Jackson's men repel the attack, but the British also suffered heavy casualties (285 killed, 1265 wounded, and 484 captured or missing) compared to light casualties for the Americans. The British forces had to break off their engagement and retreat. The odd thing about the battle was that it was unnecessary because the peace treaty (The Treaty of Ghent) had already been signed between England and the United States on December 24, 1814. However, it had not been ratified by the Senate. The battle forced the British to abide by the terms of the treaty, but Andrew Jackson gained enough fame to be positioned to become president.

The War of 1812 was costly to the United States. British troops had marched on Washington, DC, and burned the White House and the Capitol. The expansionist goals of the War Hawks were not immediately met, and territorial boundaries remained intact. The War of 1812 lasted for two years but ended without a winner. One of the ironies of the war was that by the end of the war, the main issue that caused it had been resolved. The Napoleonic Wars had ended, Napoleon had been defeated, and the British Navy had enough sailors and no longer needed to practice impressment of foreign sailors. They had also ended all trade restrictions, but this information had not reached the United States. The War of 1812 was considered a victory by the Americans, an American loss by the Canadians, and a stalemate by the British. It gave Americans a sense of unity and even gave birth to the national anthem written by Francis Scott Key.

Conclusion

The great debate over political power did not end with the signing of the US Constitution. Although the federal government would be strong and capable of taxing, waging war, and making laws, it did not satisfy everyone. The Whiskey Rebellion proved that the federal government could put down insurrections but also exposed threats to liberty. Alexander Hamilton's brilliant banking system strengthened the country's financial standing, but negatively impacted ordinary people and frontier farmers. The guarantee of religious freedom was an uneasy balance of the separation of church and state. Dissension deepened as America grappled with its place in the world and involvement in foreign wars. Although it was not adopted until after the Civil War, I cannot help but think of the Pledge of Allegiance in relation to the historical period we explored in this chapter of American history. The current version of the pledge is:

"I pledge allegiance to the Flag of the United States of America, and to the Republic for which it stands, one nation under God, indivisible, with liberty and justice for all."

Unity in America was far from reality in 1815, whether political, religious, economic, or social. Not all Americans could vote, and not all Americans were free. Yet, there was hope and momentum toward change. The sign behind my desk at home reads, "I am becoming." Our nation was becoming.

Recommended Sources

Michael Hoover. "The Whiskey Rebellion." https://www.ttb.gov/public-information/whiskey-rebellion#8.

The Lewis and Clark Expedition. https://www.history.com/topics/19th-century/lewis-and-clark.

The War of 1812. https://www.battlefields.org/learn/articles/brief-overview-war-1812.

Credits

Figure 5.1: Daniel Shays. Source: https://commons.wikimedia.org/wiki/File:Daniel_Shays_(Shays%27_Rebellion).jpg

Figure 5.2: Shays Forces Flee Continental Troops. Source: https://commons.wikimedia.org/wiki/File:Shays_forces_flee_Continental_troops,_Springfield.jpg

Figure 5.3: President George Washington. Source: https://commons.wikimedia.org/wiki/File:Gilbert_Stuart_Williamstown_Portrait_of_George_Washington.jpg

Figure 5.4: President James Madison. Source: https://commons.wikimedia.org/wiki/File:James_Madison(cropped)(c).jpg

Figure 5.5: Alexander Hamilton. Source: https://commons.wikimedia.org/wiki/File:Alexander_Hamilton_by_John_Trumbull,_1806.png

Figure 5.6: Whiskey Rebellion. Source: https://www.loc.gov/pictures/item/2002697745/

Figure 5.7: Thomas Jefferson. Source: https://www.loc.gov/pictures/item/2017660716/

Figure 5.8: Lewis and Clark with Sacajawea. Source: https://commons.wikimedia.org/wiki/File:Detail_Lewis_%26_Clark_at_Three_Forks.jpg

Figure 5.9: Siege of Fort Meigs. Source: https://commons.wikimedia.org/wiki/File:Siege_of_Fort_Meigs_by_Kellogg,_1845.jpg

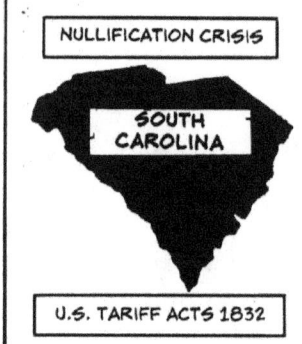

CHAPTER SIX

Building America

> Objectives
> 1. Identify the importance of infrastructure development in America in the nineteenth century.
> 2. Describe the impact of immigration in the nineteenth century on the American economy.
> 3. Understand how cotton overcame tobacco as America's leading cash crop and its impact on society.
> 4. Comprehend the complex legacy of President Andrew Jackson.

From the beginning, it seems Americans have always had ambition and grit. The United States quickly became a commercial nation, and that building process accelerated after the turn of the 19th century. Americans embraced the technology of the Industrial Revolution and integrated that into their commercial economy. Steam-powered technology drove the transportation networks and the industrial mills. This Market Revolution spread to agriculture as American farmers switched from subsistence farming to raising crops for profit. American factories emerged in numerous locations, giving rise to large cities, a new wealthy class, and a middle class. Unfortunately, the demand for slaves increased as northern textile factories were experiencing a boom cycle and needed more cotton. The unrestricted and unregulated expansion of the economy resulted in imbalances and social issues. Former subsistence farmers transitioned to factory laborers and were compelled to work extended hours for minimal wages. This led to the emergence of a new class known as the working poor, who lacked property, found themselves trapped in a never-ending cycle of poverty, and frequently had no hope for a better life.

The French Revolution and the wars between France and England increased American commerce (mainly food export). It was not expensive to transport goods across the Atlantic, but extremely expensive to transport internally by land in the United States. Americans knew they needed a national transportation infrastructure to meet the demands of their market economy. After the War of 1812, Americans built roads, canals, and railroads. The National Road, also called the Cumberland Road, was the first improved highway built by the federal government. Construction started in 1811 in Cumberland, Maryland, and eventually connected the Potomac River with the Ohio River (620 miles). President Jefferson authorized the project in 1806 to promote westward expansion. Although the National Road stimulated commercial development and improved mail and travel to the West, it was soon overshadowed by canals and railroads.

The Erie Canal was completed in 1825. The 350-mile waterway connected the Great Lakes with the Hudson River and the Atlantic Ocean. The Erie Canal carried the crops from farmers in the Great Lakes region to the eastern cities and factory goods from the East to Midwestern farmers. By 1840, more canals were being dug, including two in Ohio that connected Lake Erie to the Ohio River. Robert Fulton established scheduled steamboat service on the Hudson River by 1807, and not long after, steamboats plied the waters of the Mississippi and Ohio Rivers.

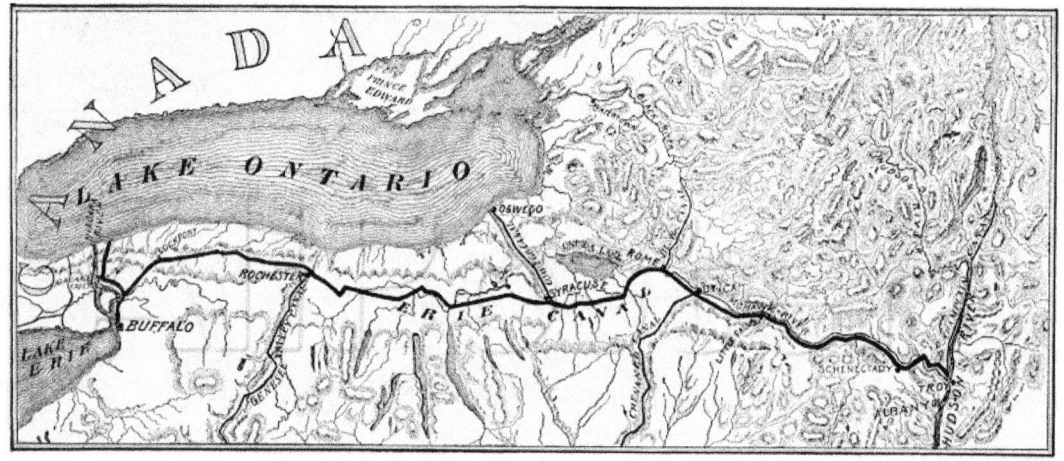

Figure 6.1: Erie Canal Map (1840)

Maryland had the first long-distance rail line in US history. The Baltimore & Ohio (B&O) Railroad Company wanted to transport agricultural products west of the Appalachian Mountains to Chesapeake Bay. Local and state governments paid for the B&O rail line, and soon after, Philadelphia, Boston, New York City, and Charleston built their rail lines. Interestingly, railroads were initially public ventures and were later taken over by private corporations. Before the Civil War, Americans had laid more than 30,000 miles of track, enabling farmers from the Midwest to quickly get their harvest to the urban centers of the East.

I was once told by a fellow historian that "lines of communication follow lines of transportation." It was certainly true regarding the railway system. Alongside the tracks were telegraph poles and wires that allowed cities to stay connected. In 1843, Samuel Morse (inventor of the Morse code) got Congress to approve the construction of a telegraph line from Baltimore to Washington, DC. During the Mexican-American War (1846-1848), telegraph lines carried battle reports from the West back to Eastern newspaper editors within a few days.

Northeastern and Midwestern farmers could produce cash crops and obtain credit from Eastern banks but were limited by a farm labor shortage. As the mother of invention, necessity drove a flurry of patents for labor-saving equipment such as Cyrus McCormick's mechanical reaper and John Deere's steel-bladed plow. With increased production, food, and transportation, cities experienced rapid growth and became filled with consumers. In 1820, New York City was the only American city with a population greater than 100,000. Thirty years later, six more American cities reached greater than 100,000. Innovative technology and the burgeoning American transportation infrastructure accounted for the growth. The Erie Canal enabled New York City to become the nation's most crucial financial and economic center, while the steamboat enabled St. Louis and Cincinnati to become trade hubs. Chicago emerged as a central railway hub tying together the Great Plains and the Great Lakes regions. American manufacturing began to migrate westward. This historical era also brought with it the rise of the corporation. Legally, corporations had privileges not afforded to ordinary citizens. Many Americans, including Thomas Jefferson, did not like the corporate takeover of business, but the Supreme Court upheld the rights of corporations in Dartmouth v. Woodward in 1819.

The Cotton Kingdom

Slave labor was the foundation of the rapid rise of the American economy. Most of the largest corporations in America in the 1830s were textile companies. Even though the Northern mills did not use slave labor, the cotton came from the South, where slave labor was the norm. The North also had slavery. For instance, in 1830, according to census data, about 3500 people were still enslaved in the North and more than 1.5 million nationwide. Southern planters expanded rapidly due to Eli Whitney's cotton gin—a hand-cranked machine that removed seeds from cotton. On a side note, one of my best friends in high school was related to Eli Whitney. He never told me if he was proud of his relative or not. Cotton was sold to national and international markets, and as demand increased, White Southern planters pushed westward beyond the Mississippi River to expand their cotton growing. Although American participation in the global slave trade ended in 1808, slave traders worked internally by moving enslaved people from the declining tobacco plantations in Virginia and North Carolina to the cotton plantations in the South and West.

From 1830 to 1861, the American South dramatically expanded its wealth and global economic influence. Cities linked to the cotton trade experienced rapid growth (such as St. Louis, New Orleans, Charleston, Mobile, and Richmond) due to global commerce. New strains of cotton were developed that would prosper further west in the country as the removal of Native Americans opened new cheap land for cultivation in the Southeastern United States. Tobacco had been the most important crop in the United States, but it was expensive, difficult to cultivate, and hard on the soil. Cotton, on the other hand, was relatively easy and inexpensive to grow. By the end of the 1830s, cotton was the most important crop in the entire country.

America's rise to power was fueled by cotton production that depended on slavery. By 1810, there were more than 1.1 million enslaved people and 2.3 million free people in the South. Slaves were a significant investment for plantation owners, who often referred to them as property. So, it is true to say that America would not be a world power today without the labor of enslaved people. The inhumanity of slavery reverberates even today. In 2021, the United States instituted a new federal holiday, Juneteenth (June 19), commemorating the ending of slavery. On June 19, 1865, Major General Gordon Granger arrived in Texas to enforce Abraham Lincoln's Emancipation Proclamation. Sadly, there were still enslaved people elsewhere, including in the North. These people did not gain their freedom until the ratification of the Thirteenth Amendment on December 6, 1865. Dear reader, it is difficult for words to convey the true horror of slavery, but I believe that watching the TV series *Roots* and the movie *Amistad* can give one a glimpse of that evil institution. Slaveholders in the South feared rebellion, as there were nearly four million slaves in the South in 1860. Thomas Jefferson wrote in his 1785 book, *Notes on the State of Virginia*:

> "It will probably be asked, why not retain and incorporate the blacks into the state, and thus save the expense of supplying, by importation of white settlers, the vacancies they will leave? Deep rooted prejudices entertained by the whites; ten thousand recollections, by the blacks, of the injuries they have sustained; new provocations; the real distinctions which nature has made; and many other circumstances, will divide us into parties, and produce convulsions which will probably never end but in the extermination of the one or the other race."

Enslaved people made up 45% of the population of the South in 1860. They created a unique culture with kinship and family structures, trade systems, and language, all under the yoke of slavery. Internal sales often broke up strong family bonds to support the cotton industry. Nat Turner, an enslaved man, was a devout Christian who was moved by what he called spirits and considered himself a prophet. Inspired by his faith, Turner led the most significant slave rebellion before the Civil War. In Southampton County, Virginia, on August 22, 1831, Turner and six others began to free enslaved people in the region. He started with his enslaver by killing him with an axe. Eventually, his group grew to over 50 individuals, and by the end of the day, the group had killed 57 men, women, and children. A militia formed the next day and successfully captured or killed all the members of Turner's group except Turner himself. Weeks later, he was captured and executed. The backlash was severe: anti-literacy and other laws related to enslaved persons were more strictly enforced, and Black churches were put under the control of White ministers.

Figure 6.2: The Capture of Nat Turner

Dear reader, reading about the evils of slavery in our history and how workers and ordinary people were mistreated in the past made me think of my parents and their experiences as immigrants in America. I would like to share that story with you now.

> I was lucky to grow up in a loving and tolerant home. My parents were hardworking immigrants who had only six years of formal education. As we read in this chapter about how America was built and prospered as a nation, I cannot help but think about all the individual people who worked hard to make a living and support their families, only to be mistreated and remain unappreciated and unknown. They sacrificed and toiled under incredible hardships to make this nation great. We owe them much gratitude.

When my parents first arrived in America in 1948, they did not speak English and had no money, but they had a dream—the American dream. They wanted to have a home, employment, peace, and freedom. Living under Nazi occupation during World War II made them appreciate everything more than most people. My mom told me she would travel through Seattle on the bus with her aunt to go shopping. My mom would speak Norwegian to her aunt, and her aunt responded:

"Be quiet! Don't speak Norwegian where others can hear you. Then they will know you are a foreigner! Just smile and nod your head." My mom thought it was odd and wondered why it would matter. Then she saw how other Norwegian immigrants were treated when they spoke their native language or attempted to speak English. They were humiliated and told to go back to wherever they came from.

My mom hated working as a maid in a rich person's home and said that the people were mean to her. My dad worked as a fisherman in Alaska and a carpenter back home in Seattle, where he worked full-time by the time I was born. He was successful and even built a six-unit apartment building. I remember I went with my dad to collect rent from a tenant. My dad knocked on the door, and the tenant opened the door and looked angry.

"Ima here to collect da rent," my dad said in his heavy Norwegian accent. The lady scowled and shot back.

"Don't bother me until you learn to speak the King's English!" she said as she poked my dad in the chest and slammed the door in his face. Another time, we went to a Christmas tree lot, selected a tree, and drove out and paid. My dad thought it was a suitable time to make a joke.

"Vi took da big vun, but da udder man said it vas free," he said again in his accented English. The lot attendant laughed out loud and then made a funny face and spoke gibberish in a mocking Scandinavian accent. As we drove away, my mom looked at my dad and said:

"You know better than to do that. They just make fun of you." My dad sat in silence.

When I was in the US Army in West Germany, my parents visited us after my first son was born. We traveled to Berchtesgaden in the southern province of West Germany known as Bavaria, where we stayed at a US Army resort for soldiers and families. The town was enchanting and picturesque. High on a mountain peak above us was the Eagle's Nest, Hitler's sanctuary. From that height, you could see Austria, where Hitler was born. We were getting a snack at what the Germans call a *schnellimbiss* (quick snack stand) when my dad wandered off. After getting our wurst (sausage) sandwiches, I turned to my mom and asked where Dad was. She pointed to a nearby bus stop. Dad talked to a group of African American soldiers, laughing and telling jokes. In 1980, in the military, it was common for soldiers to self-segregate (our barracks, for instance). I never adhered to that, but my integrated room was not the norm. My dad and the soldiers seemed to all be having a wonderful time. I waved to Dad, and he came over after shaking the hand of each Black soldier. I looked at my mom, and she said:

"All we had to do to avoid attention and not let people know we were foreigners was to stay quiet and smile. Black people cannot hide the fact they are Black. Remember," she said.

As my dad got older, he was hired by rich folks in Seattle to build their custom homes. He was doing well, and we lived a comfortable, middle-class life. One day, a rich man who had hired my father came to our house with blueprints for my dad to look over. My mom made sandwiches and coffee, as is the Norwegian custom when you have visitors. As the rich man looked around our home, he noticed a needlepoint my mom had made and hung on the wall. It depicted a basket of apples with this inscription above it: "The little apples keep all the big apples on top." The rich man smiled and pointed at my mom's creation.

"That is true," he said with a smile.

Manufacturing and Labor

Manufacturing, or the process of creating end-item goods from raw materials, propelled the United States into the pantheon of powerful nations by the turn of the 20th century. Before the manufacturing process, almost everything was custom-made. Unique, one-of-a-kind items are slow to make and expensive to buy. As impressive as the story of technological, industrial innovation is, there was a price to pay. Many Americans toiled for low wages in dangerous and unhealthy mills, factories, sweatshops, and mines.

From 1782 to 1789, inventor Oliver Evans developed continuous process flour milling, which saved labor and cut production time. In 1790, Samuel Hopkins got the first US patent (signed into law by George Washington). The US patent system was invaluable because it protected and encouraged inventors. Eli Whitney not only invented the cotton gin that made large-scale production of cotton possible but also developed the concept of interchangeable parts for manufacturing firearms (the key to mass production of all goods). Also in 1790, Samuel Slater built the first American factory in Pawtucket, Rhode Island. It was a water-powered cotton spinning mill. The demand for cotton domestically and overseas impacted the growth of industrialization in the Northeast and Midwest. The production of cloth, in turn, transformed the labor system in America. Traditionally, manufacturing laborers were involved in every stage of the production process. This was replaced by piecework, where the process was broken down into stages, with each stage completed by separate workers, sometimes even sending out the material to workers to work at home. Machines finally replaced this to make cloth, a technological process stolen from England. Industrial espionage is not new to our time; it was also standard at the turn of the 19th century.

In 1813 Francis Cabot Lowell and Paul Moody, after carefully studying textile mills in England, created their version of the power loom. Lowell also improved the manufacturing process as well (the Waltham-Lowell System). The mill in Lowell (the town named after him) was powered by the Merrimack River in northern Massachusetts. All the manufacturing took place under the same roof. Mainly, women were employed to work in harsh conditions for long hours. There were attempts to strike for better working conditions, but the ready supply of women willing to work and the appeal of the wages frustrated those attempts. Lowell's system was a momentous success, and capital flowed into New England.

Figure 6.3: Boston Manufacturing Company (1813)

The seeds of the mass production system spread to shoemaking. Shoemakers began to produce standard-sized shoes instead of custom sizes. The new manufacturing process impacted the traditional apprentice system because breaking down the process into simple steps meant manufacturers could hire unskilled workers. This new impersonal system of labor was based on class, with a growing number of low-paid, unskilled workers under the control of their capitalist bosses. The gap between the rich and poor grew ever wider.

Faced with low wages and dangerous working conditions, workers turned to the protection of unions. Labor unions in America trace their origins to the 18th century Industrial Revolution in Europe. The first recorded strike in America was in 1768 when New York journeymen tailors protested a wage reduction. Then there was the Federal Society of Journeymen Cordwainers (shoemakers) in Philadelphia in 1794. In 1825, journeymen in Boston formed a Carpenters' Union. On a personal note, my dad and brother belonged to the Carpenters' Union (part of the larger umbrella union, the AFL-CIO), and I belong to a teacher's union. Unfortunately, early American unions often excluded immigrants, women, Native Americans, and Black people.

Immigration

We owe much of our power and prestige in the world to the countless numbers of women, immigrants, slaves, and children who built America, often without any thanks, sometimes without remuneration or freedom, and under the harshest of conditions possible. Between 1820 and 1860, five million immigrants arrived in America, prompted by oppressive English laws and the infamous Irish Potato Famine. Irish immigrants, many of whom were single males, settled in the Northeast and went to work in factories and other unskilled labor jobs. German immigrants went on to rural farm areas in the Old Northwest of the United States. They usually arrived with their families. Jewish immigrants from Germany and Poland settled in urban areas where they worked in retail, commerce, and tailoring. Anti-immigrant movements were hostile to the newcomers. Nativists, native-born Anglo-Protestant Americans, wanted to limit European immigration, especially Catholics. They formed a political party in the 1850s—the Know-Nothing Party.

Immigrants joined the ranks of other industrial laborers to form unions. Those workers protected their economic power by creating closed shops—employers could only hire union workers. They also used labor strikes to help gain their demands for better working conditions and pay. Political leaders often sided with the factory, and business owners and unions did not become totally legal until the Massachusetts Supreme Court decision in 1842 made the president, but that did not solve the national conflict between labor and management. Labor activists in the 1840s organized to get a 10-hour workday and protect children in the workplace. Some states enacted laws to limit the hours that children could work and the type of work that would be prohibited for children. Women textile workers walked off the job in Lowell, Massachusetts. Despite these efforts, there was only partial success in achieving their goals of better working conditions and fewer hours.

The Jacksonian Era

Andrew Jackson was born on March 15, 1767, in the Waxhaws region of the Carolinas, which was a frontier area at the time. His parents were Scots-Irish immigrants. Jackson's father died before he was born, and he grew up in poverty and lacked much of a formal education. He overcame his life challenges and went on to become a successful attorney and a military officer. Jackson distinguished himself in the War of 1812 at the Battle of New Orleans and used that prominence to launch himself into the US presidency (1829–1837). Although he is known for shifting the American political system toward greater democracy for the people, he was no friend of the American Indian. Nicknamed "Old Hickory," three elements illustrate Andrew Jackson's importance in American history: Force of will, providence, and nature.

Andrew Jackson earned his nickname through his toughness, strength of character, and exploits as a fighter, soldier, farmer, and statesman. He came from humble beginnings and was a self-made man who was self-reliant. He believed that God guided America's democratic experiment and destiny and that he was God's right-hand man (e.g., his miraculous victory over the British in New Orleans). Jackson believed that American expansion or Manifest Destiny was natural and divinely driven. He symbolized what Americans wanted to see in themselves. Americans were closer to nature, and Jackson was a natural frontiersman. As a farmer, he understood the Jeffersonian ideal of the American yeoman farmer being the nation's backbone. Jackson's defeat of John Quincy Adams in the 1828 election was billed as the plowman beating the professor. The election of 1824 signaled the beginning of a new and more open political system—it was the end of the caucus system for choosing Republican presidential nominees. By 1824, 18 of 24 states were choosing presidential electors by popular vote. The US House of Representatives selected John Quincy Adams because Andrew Jackson (who received more popular and electoral votes than Adams) did not have the minimum required number of electoral votes.

Andrew Jackson was elected in 1828 with a popular movement behind him. His presidency seemed to herald the common man's rise because farmers and workers voted for him. He was the first president not born to comfort. During his presidency, property qualifications for voting were eliminated in most states, but not all Americans shared in Jackson's concept of rights for the common man. His mistreatment of the Cherokees best illustrated his Indian policy. Jacksonian Democracy was based on Jeffersonian Democracy and Jefferson's ideal of American yeoman farmers living in an agrarian society with limited government. Jackson feared concentrated economic power, was hostile to reform, and sought to restore old Jeffersonian virtues. As president, Jackson strengthened the executive branch but weakened the federal role in day-to-day life in America and claimed to represent the will of the people.

Nullification Crisis

Despite Andrew Jackson's belief in limited government, he was not afraid to use federal authority as the nation's chief executive. In the Nullification Crisis (1832-1833), there was a dispute between the federal government and the state of South Carolina over tariffs. The US government had imposed tariffs on British goods to protect American manufacturers. These tariffs impacted the Southern states more so than the Northern states. In 1832, South Carolina passed its South Carolina Ordinance of Nullification, which challenged the federal government's sovereignty. The protest by the government of South Carolina, led by Senator John C. Calhoun (who resigned as Jackson's vice president over the crisis), focused on the assertion that the tariffs were unconstitutional, and South Carolina even threatened to secede from the Union. President Andrew Jackson went as far as to send federal troops to South Carolina and issued a proclamation expressing his intent to preserve the Union. The crisis ended when a Compromise Tariff of 1833 was enacted. The Nullification Crisis was a dress rehearsal for the state's rights versus federal authority argument that would be one of the causes of the American Civil War.

President Jackson used the presidential veto more than any other president. He also believed in Manifest Destiny—that American expansion west was inevitable, divinely ordained, and just. In 1830, the Indian Removal Act passed with staunch support from Jackson. The act authorized the federal government to negotiate treaties with Eastern tribes who would exchange their lands for land in the West. All the costs of migration and financial aid to assist in the resettlement of the Native Americans were provided by the US government. In 1931, President Jackson used the Indian Removal Act to force a treaty with the Choctaw Tribe to remove them from the state of Mississippi.

Figure 6.4: Trail of Tears

Indian Removal and the Trail of Tears

The Cherokee are part of the Iroquoian language family of Native Americans. They may have come from the Great Lakes region and settled in Virginia, Tennessee, North Carolina, South Carolina, and Georgia. As the states expanded and their non-Indian populations grew, Native Americans were being pushed off their land. The Cherokee utilized legal avenues to protect their rights as they sought defense from settlers who were encroaching on their land by stealing their livestock, burning their towns, and squatting on their territory. In 1827, the Cherokee established a written constitution asserting their status as a sovereign nation, but Georgia refused to acknowledge their assertion of state sovereignty. The case went to the Supreme Court, but its refusal to recognize jurisdiction in Cherokee Nation v. Georgia meant that the Cherokee Nation did not have legal means to counter the Georgia laws forcing them off their land.

The Cherokee cause was considered again by the Supreme Court in Worcester v. Georgia in 1832. The Court ruled that the Cherokee nation was a foreign state and could not be subject to Georgia laws. President Jackson ignored the ruling and, using the Indian Removal Act of 1830, sent in the National Guard. The Indian Removal Act authorized the president to negotiate treaties with Native American tribes residing east of the Mississippi. These treaties required Native Americans to relinquish their lands east of the Mississippi in exchange for new lands in the West. This act affected the Southeastern nations and many others further north.

President Jackson's attitude toward Native Americans was paternalistic and patronizing—he described them as children in need of guidance. The Choctaws were the first to sign a removal treaty in September 1830. Some stayed behind, but land-hungry Whites who squatted on Choctaw territory or cheated them out of their holdings forced them out, and they moved west. Over the next 28 years, the United States government faced difficulties relocating Southeastern nations. In 1833, a small group of Seminoles was pressured into signing a removal treaty, but most of the tribe considered the treaty to be illegitimate and refused to leave. The Creeks initially refused to go, but later they signed a treaty in March 1832. This treaty opened a significant portion of their land in Alabama to non-Indian settlement while ensuring their protected ownership of the remaining portion, divided among the leading Creek families. The 1830s saw the forced removal of Native American tribes from their lands. The Creeks were cheated out of their land, leading to destitution and their forced removal. The Chickasaws signed a treaty for western land but had to pay the Choctaws to live there. The Cherokee were tricked into signing an illegitimate treaty, leading to the forced march known as the Trail of Tears. This relocation opened 25 million acres of land to non-Indian settlement and slavery.

The Cherokees had traded and intermarried with European Americans. They even adopted European customs and converted to an agricultural economy. They dressed in European clothes, built towns, and converted to Christianity. They had a written language and a formal government, and Cherokee Christians translated the Bible into their native language. Despite these efforts to assimilate, between 1721 and 1819, over 90% of their traditional land was stolen from them. However, in 1830, gold was discovered on their land, the same year that the Indian Removal Act was passed, and the state of Georgia began to sell gold mining rights to non-Indians. Cherokee were not allowed to dig for gold, conduct business, contract, or testify in court against non-Indian people.

In 1809, a Cherokee man named Sequoyah started developing a syllabary (a set of written symbols to represent each syllable in the spoken Cherokee language) to help preserve his native language and culture and promote literacy among his people. He was born in Tennessee just before the American Revolution and suffered from physical impairments. His plans to implement his written form of the Cherokee language were delayed by the War of 1812. He even volunteered to fight and took part in the Battle of Horseshoe Bend in Alabama. He struggled to develop his written language and faced accusations that he and his daughter were practicing witchcraft by putting their words on paper. The Cherokee Nation formally accepted Sequoyah's syllabary in 1825.

The Supreme Court cases involving the Cherokees touched on a more significant looming issue of state's rights. Native Americans were considered wards of the federal government and not sovereign people. However, some states wanted control over the Indians. President Martin Van Buren continued the policy of his predecessor, Andrew Jackson, and sent the US Army to march the Cherokee to Oklahoma, which had been designated Indian Territory. But the Trail of Tears story is more complicated than most of us have been led to believe.

It is easy to envision President Andrew Jackson as the villain, ordering the removal of suffering Cherokee westward or the White slaveowners pushing Native Americans off their traditional land so they could expand their plantations. This vision is complicated by the fact that some Cherokee were slaveholders themselves and that many African American slaves were also forced to march on the Trail of Tears. Also, nine presidents endorsed a top-rated plan to remove the Southeastern tribes from their land. Prominent Native leaders in all five so-called Civilized Tribes (Cherokee, Chickasaw, Choctaw, Creek, and Seminole) owned slaves, practiced slavery once they arrived in the Oklahoma Territory, and even sided with the Confederacy in the Civil War. Part of the motivation for Native Americans to enslave African Americans was the attempt to assimilate into White society. The process of Indian removal from the Southeastern United States, which claimed the lives of 11,000 Native people, was not so easy to categorize as good versus evil delineated by race, oppressor, and the oppressed, but more by human nature, which is to obtain the best deal you can, regardless of what is morally right.

Clearing out the last Civilized Tribe, the Seminoles in Florida, proved no easy task for the US government. The Seminole War of 1833 was the fiercest war waged by the US government against Native Americans. The federal government spent more than $20 million fighting the Seminoles and lost more than 1500 US soldiers. By 1842, the hostilities had ended, but no formal peace treaty had ever been signed. The precedent had been set for how the US government was going to handle Native Americans. This ugly chapter of US history would get even worse as the forces of history propelled us headlong into an inevitable Civil War.

Conclusion

From 1800–1850, America gained power due to Southern agriculture and Northern industry. A transportation infrastructure tied the nation together, and wealth accumulated quickly and propelled the United States onto the world stage. However, the economy was built on the exploitation of Native Americans, the working poor, and slaves, and many folks began to question the Founding Father's promise of liberty for all. There were cracks in the nation's façade of greatness as perhaps America's greatest crisis was on the horizon.

Recommended Sources

Eric Foner. *Free Soil, Free Labor, Free Men: The Ideology of the Republican Party Before the Civil War*.

Trail of Tears. https://www.history.com/topics/native-american-history/trail-of-tears.

Stephen B. Oates. *The Fires of Jubilee: Nat Turner's Fierce Rebellion*.

Credits

Figure 6.1: Erie Canal Map (1840). Source: https://commons.wikimedia.org/wiki/File:Erie-canal_1840_map.jpg

Figure 6.2: The Capture of Nat Turner. Source: https://commons.wikimedia.org/wiki/File:Nat_Turner_captured.jpg

Figure 6.3: Boston Manufacturing Company (1813). Source: https://commons.wikimedia.org/wiki/File:Boston_Manufacturing_Company.jpg

Figure 6.4: Trail of Tears. Source: https://commons.wikimedia.org/wiki/File:Trail_of_Tears_for_the_Creek_People_(7222969326).jpg

CHAPTER SEVEN

Reforming America

> Objectives
> 1. Describe the abolitionist movement in America and its role in the Civil War.
> 2. Identify the roots of the spiritualist movement in America and its impact on society.
> 3. Comprehend the impact of the West on the American identity.
> 4. Understand how the women's movement began in the United States.

As America approached its Civil War period, the economy expanded quickly, and the nation's power multiplied, but the problems grew commensurately as well. Corporations had too much power, women could not vote, slavery still existed, many people were turning away from traditional religion, and Native Americans had been driven off their traditional land. Still, there was a promise of a better tomorrow and some progress, although it was slow and incremental. Just as the First Great Awakening had tied the colonies together before the Revolutionary War, the Second Great Awakening hastened a reform period before the Civil War.

Figure 7.1: Camp Meeting

The Second Great Awakening was a religious revival movement that swept through America from 1795 to 1835. Mainly emanating from the Protestants, the movement manifested in meetings in cities and towns and tent revival or camp meetings in the frontier regions. During the early 1800s, church membership increased, and the focus turned toward reforms such as the temperance movement (encouraging abstinence from alcohol) and women's rights. The Awakening came in three phases: early on in Kentucky and Tennessee, spreading to New England, and then nationwide and in England. American Protestants began moving away from Calvinism (predestination) toward Arminianism (free will), named after a Dutch Reformed theologian, Jacobus Arminius.

Figure 7.2: Lucretia Mott

In a new era of reform, women began to use their traditional role of mother (paragons of virtue and morality) to project their influence onto the greater society. The Second Great Awakening and the emphasis on free will prompted this change. Women focused not only on temperance and women's rights but also on prison reform, labor laws, and the abolition of slavery. Historians have described the expectations of women in society as the "Cult of True Womanhood," protecting the morals and virtues at the home front. However, women increasingly felt empowered to exercise this moral authority to combat the moral decline of American society. Despite this more prominent role, they did not have free rein because they had no control over their property, had no legal rights to their children, could not initiate a divorce, sign legal contracts, or vote. However, there was a push to educate women to be better equipped to address society's ills. Women reformers soon realized that they could successfully link the abolition of slavery to women's rights.

In the 1830s and 1840s, the abolition movement was strong in the northern states. Lucretia Mott, a Quaker from Massachusetts who was a tireless advocate of women's rights and abolition, attended the World Anti-Slavery Convention in London. She was disappointed, however, because the organizers refused to seat her as a delegate. When she returned, she and Elizabeth Cady Stanton organized the Seneca Falls Convention in New York to address women's rights. The Seneca Falls meeting is considered the birth of the women's rights movement in America. Mott and Stanton wrote the "Declaration of Sentiments," which demanded equal rights (including voting rights) for women. Their declaration was modeled on the US Declaration of Independence while redressing women's liberty in a supposedly free society. Sixty-eight women and 32 men signed the document that called for property rights for women, equal access to all professions, and the right to vote. Despite such significant achievements in reform, the women's rights movement grew slowly and faced fierce resistance. As the Civil War became inevitable, women's rights advocates shifted their focus to the abolition of slavery.

Spiritualism

Spiritualism emerged in America around the mid-1800s and spread like wildfire. Spiritualists did not have churches or preachers. The essence of the movement was that people could communicate with the spirits of the dead through psychic mediums. The mediums would conduct séances or lead lectures in private homes or public venues where they would help people connect to their dead relatives. Full disclosure, dear reader: my mother was psychic and taught me the techniques, so my whole life has been filled with paranormal incidents, including communication with the deceased. As shocking and unbelievable as that sounds, it is true. You can check out my psychic experiences in a series of books I wrote (*Timeless, Timeless Deja Vu, Timeless Trinity, Anzar the Progenitor,* and *We Are the Aliens*). Here is a story called "Open Casket" from my first paranormal book, *Timeless: A Paranormal Personal History*.

Growing up in Seattle, my parents had many Norwegian-American friends. Almost all of them were unusual characters. One of my dad's best friends was named Asbjørn, Asbjørn Brandso. He used to work in Alaska with my dad in the 1950s. A carpenter by trade, this other Asbjørn was a highly skilled wood carver and artist. His wife, Gudrun, was quite an accomplished painter. They never had children but often accompanied us on family vacations. He was funny and could make different animal noises that fooled people. One time, we traveled to Canada with him and his wife, Gudrun. Asbjørn Brandso bought a case of Canadian whiskey and had it hidden in the trunk of his car on the way home. We stopped at the US border, and the customs agent asked if he had anything to declare.

"No! What is this? Do you think I have a trunk full of Canadian whiskey or something?!" he asked the astonished customs official. They waved him through. Another time we were camping, the people next to our campsite had a little girl. Every time the girl walked past our campsite, Asbjørn Brandso would make a strange duck noise. The girl was fascinated and hurried back to tell her parents. She returned with her parents, and they were looking through the bushes for the baby duck she swore she had heard. Asbjørn was sitting by the fire carving, and when they looked the other way, he would again make the duck noise. It was hilarious.

In February 1978, Asbjørn Brandso passed away. Mom and Dad wanted me to go to the memorial. I think it was my first funeral, and I was nervous. When we got to the funeral home in Ballard, Washington (where many Norwegians lived), there was a coffin situated in front of the mortuary chapel surrounded by flowers and a carving of a bald eagle that he had made. There he was, in an open casket. Dead. I was horrified. I hadn't been to a funeral, much less an open-casket funeral. I used to hang around graveyards when I was younger, and I even saw a dead boy who had drowned, but this was different. Now, the dead person was someone I knew. Everyone took their turn marching past the coffin and paying their last respects. Gudrun, his widow, sat by herself in a crying room behind a thinly veiled curtain. I could hear her sobbing. It was heartbreaking. Overwhelmed, I was trying to take all this in when I heard a voice.

"Don't be afraid," the voice said. It sounded like Asbjørn Brandso, but how could it be? He was dead. He was dead in a coffin right in the front of the chapel where I was sitting.

"Don't be afraid," the voice said again. Now I knew it was Asbjørn Brandso's voice. I could see his body in the coffin, and I didn't notice his body or his lips moving. His face was sunken in, and he was pale and lifeless. There is a cold stillness to death that's hard to describe unless you have seen it firsthand. You can feel it.

> "It will be okay, don't be afraid," he said in his distinctive Norwegian-American accent. I was starting to freak out but eventually could keep my cool. I wanted to say something to my mom, but I didn't.
>
> "There is nothing to be afraid of," he said, "I'm okay." Then, the voice stopped, I didn't hear anything else. I decided to walk up to the coffin and see him up close. He didn't speak to me again. I thought he was ancient, but he was only 68 years old when he died. As I type this, I'm 65 years old. Everything is relative. I can't explain how or why I heard his voice, but it was his voice from beyond death.

The spiritualist movement began in 1848, not coincidentally the same year as the Seneca Falls Convention. Many have speculated why spiritualism took root at that time, citing industrialization, urbanization, scientific breakthroughs, and rising uncertainty. It may have been all those factors coupled with the spirit of reform, but a clue could be that the spiritualist movement seems to be dominated by women. Anybody who practiced anything like spiritualism during colonial times would have been risking their life due to the puritanical view on religion. However, by the mid-1800s, America had changed rapidly due to the abovementioned reasons and the anxiety caused by immigration. Spiritualism allowed grieving families some solace while coping with the loss of loved ones. It seemed to bridge the gap between life and death, which traditional religion usually dealt with through faith alone. Simply put, America was falling apart in 1850.

In 1850, the Civil War had already begun (albeit unofficially) as pro-slavery and anti-slavery forces converged on Kansas and Missouri and began killing each other. The North had made compromises over slavery to accommodate the South, but a day of reckoning had arrived. The Second Great Awakening made more Americans aware of the evils of slavery. Although two-thirds of Americans belonged to a church, one-third did not or were looking for something else. That was the atmosphere in which spiritualism emerged. Then, in 1848, the Fox sisters from Hydesville, New York (Leah, Kate, and Maggie) learned to communicate with a spirit in their house who was making rapping or tapping noises on their walls and furniture. They would ask a question, and the spirit would answer by rapping. They became psychic mediums and held séances. News of their spirit communication spread rapidly across the country as people saw an opportunity to access what seemed like biblical powers in a time of great consternation.

There were many different types of spirit communication other than rapping. There was table tipping and direct spoken communication, and James Mansfield, known as the spiritual postmaster, could read sealed letters. People believed this because they felt these were inherently natural human abilities. There was a backlash, especially in the scientific community. Scientist Robert Hare invented a spirit device and was kicked out of his scientific society. Spiritualism was the fastest-growing movement in America in the 1850s, with well over 11 million believers (one-third of the population). As noted before, there were no organized churches or clergy and no set of standardized practices. Scientists and religious fundamentalists alike attacked spiritualism. The mid-1800s also saw the rise of other modern religions originating in the Hudson River Valley (i.e., Latter Day Saints and Seventh Day Adventists, among others). With all the revivals, religions, and spiritualism, that region of New York became known as the "burned-over district." There were some early rumblings of spiritualism before the Fox sisters, like Rachel Baker, the sleeping preacher, and Jane Rider, who could work in the dark and read books just by touching them. But by the time of the Seneca Falls Convention and Karl Marx's Communist Manifesto in 1848, the country was primed and ready for change when the Fox sisters emerged.

Figure 7.3: Mary Todd Lincoln and Abraham Lincoln's Ghost

Some other influential psychic mediums from the mid-19th century were Andrew Jackson Davis (the Poughkeepsie Seer), who wrote *The Principles of Nature*, and a British medium and women's rights advocate named Emma Hardinge Britten, who wrote *Modern American Spiritualism.* American spiritualism spread to England, and Sir Arthur Conan Doyle, famous for Sherlock Holmes, supported spiritualism. Some people began to see spiritualism as a scientific religion, especially with the help of photography (a new invention), which appeared to merge science with spirituality. William Mumler was the most famous spirit photographer of the mid-1800s. His portraits featured ghostly images near the subject of the photograph. Mary Todd Lincoln was one of his clients, and after President Lincoln's assassination, Mumler captured a photo of Lincoln's ghost standing behind Mary. Mary also held séances in the White House to communicate with her son Willy. Was it fraud or not? Never mind, it gave grieving folks comfort. Hence, its popularity grew, and such spirit photographs were published in newspapers and provided proof of life after death despite instances of trickery and manipulation.

The Fox sisters had disagreements as they grew older, and eventually, Maggie claimed that it had all been a fraud. She later recanted that confession, but the damage was already done. Despite that admission and many hoaxes by devious mediums, spiritualism survived and is reviving today. Historically, many of the same problems, doubts, and fears that folks in America had in the 1850s are present today. Some psychic mediums from that pre-Civil War era believed that spiritualism, especially that drawn from Native Americans, could heal the disharmony in the nation. Some say that another Civil War is coming. I hope not, but we should ask the spirits to be sure.

The Way West

Most Western TV shows and movies in America depict the West after the Civil War, but there was plenty of action before. After Lewis and Clark opened the West to further exploration and exploitation, fur trappers, miners, missionaries, merchants, thieves, and entrepreneurs followed. In a bizarre twist, it is odd to think that the story of the West was told mainly by the conquerors who made themselves out to be victims. Such was the narrative before 1970. The true story is much more complicated and much more interesting.

Americans began pushing toward the West as early as 1810. Pioneers used a network of trails heading West, some going all the way to the Pacific Ocean. Spurred on by Thomas Jefferson's Louisiana Purchase in 1803 and his vision of westward expansion and yeoman farmers building a great nation, the pioneers headed out on their journey west. Manifest Destiny is crucial to understanding American expansion, but even though journalist John L. O'Sullivan coined the term in the 1840s, it was not universally accepted until the 1890s. Then, it was applied to foreign expansion beyond our borders. The story of the Oregon Trail, one of the most frequented routes westward, symbolizes a time of high adventure in the West.

Oregon Trail

Over 400,000 settlers used the Oregon Trail route as they journeyed to the fruitful and abundant lands of the Pacific Northwest, seeking economic opportunity and liberty. Those individual stories of courage, hope, and promise juxtaposed the power balance turmoil over slavery and the displacement of Native peoples. The Missouri Compromise of 1820 was meant to quell the potential for further conflict by admitting Missouri as a slave state and Maine as a free state. By 1840, 40% of the US population lived west of the Appalachian Mountains. Unlike people in Europe, where industrialization and population growth had limited opportunities and created a permanent working class, Americans saw westward migration as their path to upward mobility.

Figure 7.4: Oregon Trail

The Oregon Territory was not clearly under American control until 1846. However, that did not stop fur trappers and missionaries from living in the region prior, along with many Native American tribes. Prompted by public lectures and publications, American farmers headed to Oregon, dreaming of the promised fertile land. Setting out from Independence, Missouri, in 1841, the first overland pioneers followed the old fur trapper and missionary trail to the Oregon Territory. The route followed the Platte River through the Rocky Mountains, utilizing South Pass in Wyoming and onward to the Columbia River. The settlers came to call this route the Oregon Trail. In 1842, a larger group headed West, and in 1843, over 1000 pioneers hit the Oregon Trail. The increase in numbers came from economic tough times in the Midwest and continuing promotions from folks already established in Oregon. It was a 2000-mile journey that took five to six months. Migrants would have to leave in May to make it. They would travel 12–15 miles per day. If your party left too early, there would not be enough prairie grass for the animals, and if you went too late, you would not make it through the mountain passes.

The group of pioneers in 1843 comprised men, women, children, and approximately 5000 oxen and cattle. They followed a missionary as their guide. Although the Great Plains were relatively flat, the river crossings could be treacherous. One of the biggest fears for the migrants was an attack by Native Americans. The well-publicized Whitman Massacre, in what is now near Walla Walla, Washington, in 1847, was prompted by a measles outbreak that the Native tribes blamed on the Missionaries Marcus and Narcissa Whitman. Such attacks would occasionally take place, but the far greater danger for settlers headed west were diseases like cholera, smallpox, and flu, and accidents such as accidental discharge of firearms, falling off horses or mules, runaway wagons in the mountains, and drowning in river crossings. Ten percent of the pioneers died along the way. It is said that there are 10 graves for every mile along the trail. Large convoys of wagons eventually gave way to many smaller groups later.

The trip along the Oregon Trail required great forethought and planning. Most pioneers had to sell their homes, businesses, and possessions. They also had to buy six months' worth of provisions (flour, sugar, bacon, coffee, salt, firearms, and ammunition). The most popular method of conveyance was the smaller prairie schooner wagon (not the Conestoga wagon depicted in many films). The wagons, which were six feet wide and 12 feet long, were covered with oiled canvas stretched over a wooden frame. At the peak of the Oregon Trail's popularity, during the 1849 California Gold Rush, there were thousands of people on the trail at the same time. Independence Rock in Wyoming was the halfway point; if the migrants reached the landmark by July 4, they were on schedule. On a personal note, my wife Ginger and I stopped at Independence Rock and saw the names of countless pioneers who had chiseled their names into the rock. Once the settlers reached Fort Laramie, Wyoming, they began their arduous ascent through the Rocky Mountains. Eventually, they reached the Snake River Canyon and another climb over the Blue Mountains before finally reaching the Columbia River, the settlements in the Dalles or Oregon City. Some folks continued to California. With the completion of the first transcontinental railroad in 1869, the migration by wagons decreased dramatically. Today, you can still see the wagon ruts carved into the sandstone along the Oregon Trail in some places.

The Mexican-American War

The Missouri Compromise did not end the conflict over slavery. New territories that were not part of the Louisiana Purchase were not part of the agreement. Because the Southern economy depended on cotton and the plantation owners needed free labor to grow cotton, the issue of slavery's expansion would not go away as some in the North had hoped. Not only did Americans settle in Oregon, but they also migrated to California, New Mexico, and Texas. The famous Battle of the Alamo occurred from February 23 to March 6, 1836, in San Antonio, Texas. The Alamo was a Spanish mission made into a fort with 100 folks guarding it. President General Antonio López de Santa Anna attacked the Alamo for nearly two weeks and eventually killed most of the defending Texas forces. Driven by revenge (Remember the Alamo), Texans rallied and defeated the Mexican Army at the Battle of San Jacinto on April 21, 1836.

In 1837, American settlers in Texas got their independence from Mexico and sought admission as a slave state. Pro-slavery President James K. Polk facilitated Texas joining the union as a slave state in 1846 and Oregon as a free state. Polk then declared war on Mexico after claiming that the Mexican Army had invaded American territory. Many people were against the war, believing that it was a ploy to expand the power of the slave states.

Figure 7.5: Battle of Molino del Rey

The Mexican-American War was fought between the United States and Mexico between 1846 and 1848. After Texas gained its independence from Mexico, the United States annexed Texas in 1845, escalating tensions between the two countries. Mexico claimed that the Texas border ended at the Nueces River, while the United States claimed it ended at the Rio Grande River. On April 25, 1846, Mexican troops attacked US soldiers in the border area under dispute. General Zachary Taylor defeated Mexican forces at the Battle of Palo Alto (May 8, 1846) and Resaca de la Palma (May 9, 1846). Later, at the Battle of Molino del Rey on September 8, 1847, the bloodiest battle of the Mexican-American War occurred on the outskirts of the Mexican capital. It was part of the Battle for Mexico City, which the Americans captured one week later. Ulysses S. Grant served as a captain during this battle, which became a significant turning point in the war.

After two years of war and several American victories, the Treaty of Guadalupe Hidalgo was signed on February 2, 1848. Mexico ceded territories that would eventually become the states of Texas, California, Nevada, Utah, New Mexico, Arizona, and parts of Colorado and Wyoming. Gold was discovered in California shortly after the war ended.

The Compromise of 1850

The US victory in the Mexican-American War left the status of newly won territory in question. Would slavery be allowed or not? Kentucky Senator Henry Clay proposed a new compromise: California would enter the Union as a free state, the status of slavery in the remaining former Mexican territory would be left up to those who lived there, the slave trade (although not slavery itself) would be banned, and a new Fugitive Slave Act would enable Southern slave owners to reclaim runaway slaves in the North. The Gadsden Purchase in 1853 added another 30,000 square miles of Mexican territory to the United States (Southwestern New Mexico and Southern Arizona) at a cost of $10 million to Mexico and completed the south border as it stands today.

Bleeding Kansas

Bleeding Kansas, also known as the Border War, was a period of violent conflict between pro-slavery and anti-slavery forces in the Kansas Territory between 1855 and 1859. In 1854, Illinois Senator Stephen A. Douglas proposed that the new states of Kansas and Nebraska be established. They would be free states because they were north of the demarcation line at 36°30' parallel. To avoid a Southern veto, he suggested that the people of Nebraska and Kansas should be allowed to choose for themselves whether to allow slavery. It did not take long for pro-slavery and anti-slavery forces to descend on Kansas, ready to fight. Thousands of new migrants from both slave and free states rushed into Kansas to influence the vote, eventually leading to mayhem, chaos, and a mini-civil war that served as a dress rehearsal for the American Civil War—armed conflict over slavery seemed inevitable.

The Mormons

In 1816, when he was only 11 years old, Joseph Smith's family moved to Western New York state. Four years later, he started having a series of visions. The Second Great Awakening was happening in the Hudson River Valley at that time, and religious revivals were quite common in the area. In the first vision, he claimed that he saw God the Father and Jesus Christ. Three years later, in 1823, he saw an angel named Moroni who guided him to a buried book of golden plates containing a Judeo-Christian history of an ancient American civilization written by a Native American prophet named Mormon in the fifth century. Smith published a translation of the golden plates in his Book of Mormon in 1830. He also organized the Church of Christ (later changed to the Church of Jesus Christ of Latter-Day Saints), saying that he had restored the original Christian Church. Church members are now known as Latter-Day Saints or Mormons. Converts took on missionary roles and spread the message of the Book of Mormon throughout America and eventually overseas. The Mormons were forced to move many times—from New York to Ohio, to Missouri, to Illinois, where they built a community on the Mississippi River called Nauvoo. The Mormons faced further criticism when Smith and some others took many wives, practicing polygamy. Joseph Smith was murdered by a mob in 1844. That same year, Brigham Young took over as leader and, in 1846, led the Mormons to the Great Salt Lake, a 1300-mile journey.

Figure 7.6: Assassination of Joseph Smith

The California Gold Rush

So many key events in American history happened in 1848 (i.e., the Seneca Falls Convention, the start of the Spiritualism, and the end of the Mexican-American War), not the least of which was the discovery of gold at Sutter's Mill on the American River in California. More than 300,000 fortune seekers came to California from 1848 to 1852. Few could strike it rich except those who sold provisions to the miners; they fared well. Prospectors (known as 49ers) came from all over the world to find gold. California's cities grew rapidly, especially San Francisco. The Gold Rush stimulated the economy and led to infrastructure development. It also served as a melting pot of diverse cultures—Americans, Europeans, Chinese, Mexicans, and many others. Women capitalized on the bustling economy as entrepreneurs, cooks, boardinghouse owners, and merchants. The story of the Gold Rush also cemented the legacy of the West as a place of high risk and high reward and placed a heavy burden on the environment as gold panning in rivers eventually gave way to even more destructive methods. All the attention, population, and economic growth led to California becoming a state in 1850 and bringing the issue of slavery to the forefront because of westward expansion and the battle for political power.

Figure 7.7: Gold Mining in 1850

The Transcendentalists

Beginning in New England, Transcendentalism was a 19th-century American philosophical and literary movement characterized by a profound belief in individualism, self-reliance, and a deeper spiritual connection to the natural world. The movement was influenced by the Vedas (ancient Indian scriptures), British writers like Samuel Taylor Coleridge and William Wordsworth, and the German Romantics like Johann Wolfgang von Goethe, Wilhelm Heinrich Wackenroder, and Friedrich Wilhelm Joseph Schelling, among others. The Transcendentalists believed in a direct connection to God, opposed materialism, embraced idealism, and saw nature as a source of spiritual insight. The most important American Transcendentalists, Ralph Waldo Emerson, Henry David Thoreau, and Margaret Fuller, helped form America's first distinctive philosophy and literature.

Figure 7.8: Margaret Fuller

Transcendentalists challenged organized religion, celebrated individuality, stood for women's rights, and supported the abolition of slavery. Emerson is often seen as the founder who laid the groundwork for the movement, as expressed in his essays "Self-Reliance" and "Nature." Henry David Thoreau experimented with simple natural living at Walden Pond, Massachusetts, and wrote *Walden, or Life in the Woods*. He also wrote an essay, "Resistance to Civil Government," that expressed Transcendentalist ideals of self-reliance through individual rights in self-government. Margaret Fuller was the key female Transcendentalist who advocated for women's rights and intellectual freedom. She wrote the first major feminist work in America—*Woman in the Nineteenth Century*.

Transcendentalists believed people could attain spiritual truth through intuition and personal experience and bypass traditional religious institutions. They sought communion with nature because they considered the natural world a teacher and reflective of the divine spirit. Although not anti-capitalist per se, they did stress the importance of personal growth and self-discovery. Because of their emphasis on individualism, Transcendentalists also advocated for the end of slavery and supported rights for women in addition to education system reform. They challenged what they considered to be unjust laws and oppressive institutions. Their influence was felt in forming a uniquely American identity of self-reliance, nonconformity, and fearless pursuit of truth, and the modern environmental movement owes much to the Transcendentalists and Thoreau's call to live deliberately and harmoniously with nature.

Abolitionism

Several movements worked in conjunction in the pre-Civil War era (antebellum). The women's rights advocates, spiritualists, revivalists, and transcendentalists all favored the end of slavery. Inspired by the Second Great Awakening in the 1830s, religious leaders like William Lloyd Garrison, Arthur and Lewis Tappan, Dwight Weld, and Quakers Lucretia Mott and John Greenleaf Whittier called for immediate emancipation instead of the earlier push to re-patriate American slaves to Africa. They sought to persuade enslavers to voluntarily release their slaves in an appeal to their Christian conscience. In 1831, Garrison established the newspaper *The Liberator*, spearheading a campaign to promote immediate emancipation and citizenship for Black people in America. He presided over the American Anti-Slavery Society, calling to action reformers to save the nation by ending slavery. To fully understand its evolution, let us look back at the history of abolitionism.

Figure 7.9: The Liberator

An abolitionist was a person who believed that slavery in the United States should end immediately. With the writing of the Constitution, some of the Founding Fathers, like Thomas Jefferson, attempted to put antislavery language in an early draft (even though he held slaves himself). This attempt was not successful due to protests from the Southern colonies. Benjamin Franklin, who was also a slaveholder, was a member of one of the first antislavery organizations in the United States—the Pennsylvania Society for the Abolition of Slavery.

Following the Revolutionary War, the Northern states began to abolish slavery, completing the task by 1804. Many individual slaveholders in the Upper South made provisions in their wills to free their slaves, supposedly moved by the revolutionary ideals of equality expressed in the Declaration of Independence and the US Constitution. The percentage of free black people in the Upper South increased from less than 1% to nearly 10% from 1790 to 1810. President Thomas Jefferson signed the Act Prohibiting the Importation of Slaves in 1807, and he privately supported the Missouri Compromise in 1820, which prohibited slavery north of 36°30' North, excluding Missouri.

William Lloyd Garrison founded the American Anti-Slavery Society in 1833. The Virginia legislature debated abolition from 1829 to 1831, and in the North, there were serious discussions about freeing slaves and sending them to Africa for settlement. This led to the founding of Liberia as an African country. Between 1822 and the end of the Civil War, more than 15,000 freed and free-born Black Americans settled in Liberia (which declared its independence in 1847).

Nat Turner, born a slave, led a rebellion of slaves in Virginia in August 1831. More than 80 slaves joined in, and they murdered 60 White people. There were several slave rebellions between 1776 and 1865, but Turner's was the most violent and had the most significant impact. As a result of the uprising, pro-slavery forces tightened their grip on the slaves, and antislavery forces noted that only more blood would spill until slavery was abolished. Congress passed the Fugitive Slave Law in 1850, which made it illegal to assist runaway slaves, even in the North. This law made the Northern states complicit with slavery in the South and further divided the nation. In the 1850s, the 15 states that constituted the American South still supported slavery, especially in the agricultural areas and less so in the border states and urban areas. In 1860, there were four million slaves in the United States.

On March 6, 1857, the U.S. Supreme Court decided that slave owners had the right to take their slaves into Western territories. The most critical issue of the 1850s was whether slavery should be allowed in the West. The Compromise of 1850 allowed new territories to decide for themselves on the issue of slavery by popular vote. When this process was tested in Kansas, violence broke out. Dred Scott was a slave whose owner had lived in Illinois (which was a free state) and Wisconsin, which was a free territory when Scott lived there. The court ruled that Scott was not free based on his residence because he was not considered a person under the law. Scott was his owner's property, which could not be taken away without due process of law. The justices were trying to end the debate about slavery in the West and overlooked the fact that many free Black people were living in the North.

Figure 7.10: Dred Scott

Former slave Frederick Douglass, free Blacks Charles Henry Langston and John Mercer Langston (brothers), William Lloyd Garrison, and Harriet Beecher Stowe were all leading abolitionists in the North. When President Lincoln was introduced to author Stowe, he allegedly said: "So you're the little woman who wrote the book that made this great war!" Her novel *Uncle Tom's Cabin* was published in 1852 and served to galvanize the abolitionist movement.

Uncle Tom's Cabin was intended to educate people about the horrors of slavery. Stowe showed that slavery impacted everyone in America, including people in the North, and hoped to change hearts and minds in the South as well. Although *Uncle*

Tom's Cabin did, unfortunately, popularize some stereotypes of Black people, it also proved that literature can be an agent of social change.

Frederick Douglass was a famous American abolitionist, statesman, speaker, and author. He escaped slavery at age twenty, and his three autobiographical books are essential reading in American history. Douglass was born into slavery around 1818 in Maryland. He became one of America's most famous intellectuals of the latter nineteenth century. He was an advisor to presidents and lectured on various topics, including women's rights. He died on February 20, 1895. Douglass said, "No man can put a chain about the ankle of his fellow man without at last finding the other end fastened about his own neck." This quote truly captures the spirit of the antislavery movement. Not only was slavery harmful to the slave, but it was also harmful to the slave owner and the country. Douglass was probably the most distinguished and eloquent speaker regarding the evils of slavery. His words ring as true today as they did over 150 years ago. "Where justice is denied, where poverty is enforced, where ignorance prevails, and where any one class is made to feel that society is an organized conspiracy to oppress, rob, and degrade them, neither persons nor property will be safe."

John Brown did not believe in a slow evolutionary approach to ending slavery; he believed in the violent overthrow of the slavery system. Brown took part in the antislavery conflicts in Kansas and thought that he and his sons were doing the will of God. By 1858, he had recruited more radical abolitionists bent on creating a slave rebellion. In 1859, Brown and nearly two dozen of his followers attacked and took over a federal arsenal at Harpers Ferry in Virginia. He intended to seize weapons and supplies to support his planned slave rebellion. He was not successful, and several were killed, including most of his men and his two sons. The US Marines, under the command of Robert E. Lee, put down the uprising. John Brown was captured and sentenced to death for murder, inciting slave insurrection, and treason. After sentencing, Brown pronounced, "If it is deemed necessary that I should forfeit my life for the furtherance of the ends of justice, and mingle my blood further with the blood of my children and with the blood of millions in this slave country whose rights are disregarded by wicked, cruel, and unjust enactments—I submit; so let it be done!" John Brown was hanged on December 2, 1859, after allegedly passing on these final words in a note, "I, John Brown, am now quite certain that the crimes of this guilty land will never be purged away but with blood."

Figure 7.11: John Brown

Many textbooks portray Brown as a villain and a madman who went crazy and turned into a murdering extremist. Since the 1970s, however, most history books have taken a fresh look at this highly committed and complicated man. Frederick Douglass offered this: "His zeal in the cause of my race was far greater than mine—it was as the burning sun to my taper light—mine was bounded by time, his stretched away to the boundless shores of eternity. I could live for the slave, but he could die for him." American novelist Herman Melville called him "the meteor of the war."

Conclusion

The antebellum reform movements were diverse and impactful. The Second Great Awakening was the springboard for many movements of the 1800s. It led to a spiritualist movement that encouraged people to look beyond everyday reality and expand their consciousness. It also helped foster the Transcendentalists who asked us to focus on the natural world and the importance of the individual. Abolitionists caused us to question and condemn the national compromise that allowed the evil of slavery to continue after the American Revolution. The westward expansion helped Americans search for economic opportunity, freedom, and liberty but also inflicted harm on Native Americans in the process. Finally, the equal treatment of women in

American society was addressed through the women's rights movement. We all know that the Civil War came next after all these attempts at reform, both some successes and some catastrophic failures. In this chapter, dear reader, we have seen that America had came to a crossroads. The Civil War, despite reforms, could be seen as a failure, or it could be seen as a natural part of the growth of all great nations, as growth often comes from conflict and loss. The reforms were not without purpose or a positive effect, as many positive developments after the Civil War had been proposed and established before the war. A foundation of reform had been established so that the world could later assess how America treated its women, ethnic minorities, Indigenous people, immigrants, and the working class. As we all know, there is still much work to be done.

Recommended Sources

Ann Braude. *Radical Spirits: Spiritualism and Women's Rights in Nineteenth-Century America.*

Richard White. *A New History of the American West, "It's Your Misfortune and None of My Own."*

The Mexican-American War. https://www.history.com/topics/19th-century/mexican-american-war.

Credits

Figure 7.1: Camp Meeting. Source: https://loc.gov/pictures/resource/ds.03095/

Figure 7.2: Lucretia Mott. Source: https://commons.wikimedia.org/wiki/File:Lucretiamott2.jpg

Figure 7.3: Mary Todd Lincoln and Abraham Lincoln's Ghost. Source: https://commons.wikimedia.org/wiki/File:Mumler_(Lincoln).jpg

Figure 7.4: Oregon Trail. Source: https://commons.wikimedia.org/wiki/File:Albert_Bierstadt_Oregon_Trail.jpg

Figure 7.5: Battle of Molino del Rey. Source: https://commons.wikimedia.org/wiki/File:Battle_Molino_del_Rey.jpg

Figure 7.6: Assassination of Joseph Smith. Source: https://commons.wikimedia.org/wiki/File:Assassination-of-joseph-smith-carthage.jpg

Figure 7.7: Gold Mining in 1850. Source: https://commons.wikimedia.org/wiki/File:1850_Woman_and_Men_in_California_Gold_Rush.jpg

Figure 7.8: Margaret Fuller. Source: https://commons.wikimedia.org/wiki/File:FullerDaguerreotype.jpg

Figure 7.9: The Liberator. Source: https://commons.wikimedia.org/wiki/File:The_Liberator_masthead,_1861_Jan_11.jpg

Figure 7.10: Dred Scott. Source: https://commons.wikimedia.org/wiki/File:Dred_Scott_photograph_(circa_1857).jpg

Figure 7.11: John Brown. Source: https://commons.wikimedia.org/wiki/File:184647_John_Brown_by_Augustus_Washington_(without_frame).jpg

CHAPTER EIGHT

Dividing America

> Objectives
> 1. Understand the causes of the Civil War.
> 2. Comprehend the strategy used by Abraham Lincoln to win the war.
> 3. Compare the strengths and weaknesses of both the North and the South.
> 4. Define the legacies of the Civil War.

> *In your hands, my dissatisfied fellow-countrymen, and not in mine, is the momentous issue of civil war. The Government will not assail you. You can have no conflict without being yourselves the aggressors. You have no oath registered in heaven to destroy the Government, while I shall have the most solemn one to "preserve, protect, and defend it." I am loath to close. We are not enemies, but friends. We must not be enemies. Though passion may have strained it must not break our bonds of affection. The mystic chords of memory, stretching from every battlefield and patriot grave to every living heart and hearthstone all over this broad land, will yet swell the chorus of the Union, when again touched, as surely they will be, by the better angels of our nature.*
>
> —Abraham Lincoln, Inaugural Address, March 1861

I could think of no better way to start this chapter, dear reader, than to share the words of Abraham Lincoln. Not only did his carefully chosen words so succinctly and accurately capture the country's mood in 1861, but they also do so today. Lincoln's inaugural speech was a warning to the South, but it also offered an alternative to war. In most of the histories written on the Civil War, the authors begin with the Confederate forces' attack on Fort Sumter in Charleston Bay, South Carolina. Still, unofficially, the war had already started in the West. Westward expansion spurred conflict between pro-slavery and antislavery forces in Kansas. Also, the Fugitive Slave Law of 1850 tacitly made the North support slavery in the South. The southern states knew that abolitionists were gaining momentum, and that Abraham Lincoln was leading the charge, so they steadily accepted what they considered to be the inevitability of civil war. The American Revolution, unfortunately, had left two vital questions unanswered: Was the United States a confederation of sovereign states, and would slavery continue to exist? By the time the Civil War was over, it had claimed nearly 700,000 lives, more than all other American wars combined.

Figure 8.1: Abraham Lincoln

The North and the South could not agree on handling the country's expansion in the West. Lincoln promised to stop the growth of slavery in those Western territories. When Lincoln was elected, the Southern states saw no alternative but to secede from the Union. The South formed a new country, the Confederate States of America, which most people in the North did not recognize and supported President Lincoln's efforts to preserve the Union. The Confederate Army attacked Fort Sumter on April 12, 1861, and by the end of the year, one million American soldiers had been deployed on the battlefield to fight each other.

Here is an essential summary of critical points to consider while studying the American Civil War:
1. Initially, the North went to war to preserve the Union, not to end slavery.
2. The South fought for states' rights to preserve slavery.
3. Western expansion was a critical factor in igniting the Civil War.
4. Most of the war was fought in the South.

5. More than three million men fought in the war.
6. Nearly 2% of the American population died in the war. That same percentage today would amount to 7.5 million dead.
7. African Americans (only 1% of the Northern population) made up 10% of the Union Army.
8. The words "In God We Trust" first appeared on US money in 1864.
9. Officially, the Civil War started April 12, 1861, at Fort Sumter, South Carolina, and ended April 9, 1865, at Appomattox Courthouse, Virginia.
10. Many battlefield wounds were treated by traumatic amputations, some without anesthesia.
11. Most generals knew each other and went to military academies together.
12. The Emancipation Proclamation (January 1863) transformed the Civil War into a war to restore the Union *and* end slavery.
13. Ironically, the Confederate government under President Jefferson Davis abandoned the concept of states' rights and became even more federalized than the US government.

State's Rights

Many history textbooks after the Civil War tended to downplay the evils of slavery and the intent of the South. They used names for the Civil War, such as "the War Between the States" or even the bizarre "War of Northern Aggression." The issue, according to those outdated and incorrect textbooks, was states' rights, not slavery. During the constitutional phase of American history after the Revolutionary War, the Southern states demanded the Bill of Rights (the first 10 amendments) because they feared a strong centralized government. Southerners believed that protecting states' rights would preserve individual rights and protect their "property" (which was how they often referred to their slaves). Of course, an exception was made not to consider slavery when discussing individual rights. The concept of states' rights arises from that fundamental argument over the federal government's power vis-à-vis the states. The Founding Fathers were divided on the issue of states' rights and fell into two opposing camps: Federalists and Anti-Federalists. John Adams, Alexander Hamilton, Benjamin Franklin, George Washington, and James Madison were all Federalists. Thomas Jefferson, Thomas Paine, Richard Henry Lee, Patrick Henry, and Samuel Adams were all Anti-Federalists.

There was a warning sign for the Civil War during the Nullification Crisis of 1832–1833 when South Carolina challenged the federal government over federal tariffs. South Carolina held that it had the right to overturn any federal law deemed harmful to its state. Andrew Jackson stepped in and quelled the crisis, but the haunting legacy of Anti-Federalism continued to rise to the surface. Many people in the North believed that the market economy would eventually destroy slavery as a viable institution. Still, the South stubbornly clung to slavery and realized that the westward expansion of slave-owning states would be essential to promote their cause. As soon as Abraham Lincoln was elected, seven Southern states seceded from the union. When Lincoln called in the troops, four more states in the South seceded. The first state to secede was South Carolina.

Figure 8.2: The First Battle of Bull Run

First Bull Run (1861)

The reality of war set in when the North and the South squared off in Manassas, Virginia. The South was victorious in the First Battle of Manassas on July 21, 1861. The North referred to the battle as Bull Run. More than 35,000 Union troops attacked a smaller (20,000) Confederate force intending to capture Richmond, the Southern capital. About 25 miles into their march, General P.G.T. Beauregard encountered the Union Army, and with the help of reinforcements in the afternoon, the Confederates broke the Union's right flank, and the Union was forced to retreat. Whatever illusions Northern leadership had of a quick, decisive victory in the war were dashed.

Figure 8.3: The Battle of Shiloh

The Battle of Shiloh

The North and the South fought the Battle of Shiloh from April 6 to April 7, 1862. Also known as the Battle of Pittsburg Landing, the fight occurred in southwestern Tennessee. The opposing commanders were General Albert Sidney Johnston of the Confederate forces and Major General Ulysses S. Grant of the Union Army. Grant hoped to capture a vital Confederate railway hub in northern Mississippi. The South did well on the first day of fighting, taking the Union troops by surprise before the planned arrival of Union General Don Carlos Buell and his reinforcement troops, but General Johnston was mortally wounded. When the Union counterattacked the second day in full force, the Confederates retreated, and General Grant claimed victory. The Battle of Shiloh was one of the bloodiest battles of the Civil War, with more than 24,000 soldiers killed.

The Battle of Antietam

Also known as the Battle of Sharpsburg, the Battle at Antietam occurred on September 17, 1862, near Sharpsburg, Maryland, along Antietam Creek. Confederate General Robert E. Lee planned to bring the battle to the North by splitting his forces—some would move into Pennsylvania to threaten Washington, DC, and some would move supplies into Maryland. Major General George B. McClellan marched his Union troops to confront General Lee at Antietam. Unfortunately, General

McClellan (an overly cautious man) waited 18 hours to move his forces against General Lee, giving the Confederates time to reinforce and dig in defensive positions. Although the battle stopped General Lee's invasion of Washington, DC, President Lincoln was upset with General McClellan for hesitancy in battle and reluctance to pursue the Confederates as they fled south. The Battle of Antietam was the bloodiest day in US war history, with nearly 23,000 dead, wounded, or missing on both sides.

Figure 8.4: General Robert E. Lee

Naval Battles of the Civil War

Civil War naval battles were significant and influenced the future of naval warfare. The first such battle was the Battle of Hampton Roads, also known as the Battle of the Monitor and Merrimack (which had been rebuilt and renamed as the CSS Virginia) or the Battle of Ironclads. From March 8 to March 9, 1862, located at the estuary where the Elizabeth and Nansemond Rivers meet the James River and enter the Chesapeake Bay near Norfolk, Virginia, the two ironclads met for battle. The Confederacy wanted to break the Union blockade that had cut them off from international trade. The Confederate ship, the CSS Virginia, was about to attack a

Union ship when the USS Monitor, an ironclad Union ship, arrived. The clash between the two ironclads lasted three hours, with neither side inflicting enough damage on the other. The battle ended indecisively but is significant because it was the first battle between ironclad ships in history. Later, in April 1862, the Union Navy helped capture the City of New Orleans, and in 1864, at the Battle of Cherbourg, the USS Kearsarge sank the Confederate ship CSS Alabama. The Confederacy also developed a human-powered submarine, the CSS H.L. Hunley, which successfully sank the Union ship USS Housatonic. These naval engagements marked a turning point in naval tactics and technology that would influence future American wars at sea.

Figure 8.5: Battle of the Ironclads

The Emancipation Proclamation

President Lincoln knew that the Civil War was about ending slavery, but political pragmatism prompted him first to make it a war to restore the Union. He knew that one-third of the nation favored abolition, one-third did not, and one-third were on the fence. You cannot lead when people will not follow, so Lincoln had to be patient. On January 1, 1863, he issued the Emancipation Proclamation, freeing the slaves in the South. Some have criticized Lincoln for not initially making emancipation the reason for the war and for freeing slaves in a country (the Confederate States of America) that was not under his control. Still, they are missing the fact that politics is the art of the possible. Regardless, the Emancipation Proclamation brought hope to enslaved people, and many Black people escaped to the North so they could join the Union Army. By June 19, 1865 (now a federal holiday known as Juneteenth), the Union Army controlled all Confederate territory and had liberated all slaves. President Lincoln had convinced the North that ending slavery was in everyone's best interest and the right and moral thing to do. Black soldiers volunteering to fight for the Union also convinced many folks in the North that the war had a higher purpose.

The 54th Massachusetts Infantry

The 1989 movie *Glory*, starring Denzel Washington, Morgan Freeman, and Matthew Broderick, tells the story of the 54th Massachusetts Infantry. I recommend this movie to everyone, especially those studying American history. One month after Lincoln issued the Emancipation Proclamation, Governor John A. Andrew of Massachusetts called for the formation of the 54th Massachusetts Infantry Regiment. One thousand Black soldiers from Massachusetts and other states (including Southern states) enlisted. Frederick Douglass had two sons in the regiment. Prevailing prejudices did not allow Black people to become officers, so Colonel Robert Gould Shaw was put in command. At one point, as a sign of respect and honor, the White officers and non-commissioned officers refused to take any pay unless everyone was paid the same regardless of race. The regiment fought bravely at Fort Wagner near Charleston, South Carolina, on July 18, 1863. The 54th lost half of their men in that battle, including Colonel Shaw. They were all buried together in a mass grave by the Confederates who defended Fort Wagner. The Confederate forces intended burying Colonel Shaw with his Black troops would be an insult, but Shaw's parents refused an offer to move Shaw's body to an officers' cemetery. Colonel Shaw's father told everyone that his son should be left in the place of honor with his men. Dear reader, if you do not mind, I would like to share a personal story inspired by teaching experiences that relate to these topics.

Figure 8.6: The Storming of Fort Wagner

Before I knew I would be a history professor, I was interested in the Civil War. I had Civil War army men that I played with, and I watched a few movies like *Major Dundee*, *The Horse Soldiers*, *The Red Badge of Courage*, and *Sergeant Rutledge* on Saturday afternoons growing up in a peaceful middle-class life in the Seattle suburbs. *Sergeant Rutledge* was set in the post-Civil War era out West, but it dealt skillfully with racism, especially for a film in 1960. It was hard for me to understand why there was racial hatred and why Americans fought each other in the Civil War. I understood World War II because my parents lived under Nazi occupation in Norway, and all Americans fought a foreign enemy together. But I knew enough to know that the Civil War was about slavery.

When I joined the US Army in 1978, I met a diverse contingent of soldiers from every part of the United States, including the South. We only had two Black people in my high school, but nearly one-quarter of my fellow GIs were African American. It was quite a culture shock for me as I learned about their experiences growing up that seemed similar in some ways to my experiences and quite different in other ways. During basic training, I was called a "Yankee" for the first time and was shocked to meet a Ku Klux Klan (KKK) member when I arrived for my assignment in West Germany. He even showed me a membership card. Some of the Southern soldiers displayed Confederate flags in our barracks, and most of the barrack's rooms were segregated by race (mine was integrated). Any mention of the Civil War was met with hostility from most White soldiers from the South. The legacy of the Civil War and the issues surrounding that war became increasingly clear to me.

During my job interview at Citrus in 1998, I was asked about Little Round Top, the key fight during the Battle of Gettysburg. Luckily, my interest in the Civil War since childhood prepared me for the question. I explained that a professor of rhetoric and oratory from Bowdoin College named Colonel Joshua Chamberlain, who volunteered for the Union Army, won the battle with a brilliant maneuver called the "swinging gate" bayonet charge.

Confederate General George E. Pickett led an unsuccessful charge up to Colonel Chamberlain's position at Little Round Top via Devil's Den (a peculiar rock formation) and the Valley of Death. I was also familiar with another remarkable story about an African American woman named Lydia Hamilton Smith within the larger story of Gettysburg. She provided food and clothing to both Union and Confederate troops. I knew about the significant contributions of Black soldiers in the Union Army and the leadership of Frederick Douglass, a former slave and civil rights leader who became a US senator after the war. My interest in the subject, real-world experiences in the Army, and a loving and tolerant upbringing combined to help me deftly handle the hiring committee's question.

What continues to amaze me is that in a time of such terrible hatred, carnage, death, and inhumanity, some individual Americans rose to the occasion to operate with great courage, morality, and wisdom in a cause that they knew was righteous. As noble as that sentiment is, war itself is a form of madness, and as President Lyndon B. Johnson said in the 20th century, "War is killing a man you don't even know well enough to hate." My wish for us as a nation and as individuals is to be strong and just as we navigate a world filled with hate, greed, and intolerance.

The Battle of Gettysburg

The Gettysburg battlefield is one of the most haunted sites in America. And it is no wonder because the number of casualties from that battle is staggering. The battle raged from July 1 to July 3, 1863. Abraham Lincoln was worried when the generals he chose to replace General McClellan failed to achieve victories at Fredericksburg, Virginia (December 1862), and Chancellorsville, Virginia (May 1863, where General Thomas J. "Stonewall" Jackson was killed). General Robert E. Lee took these two Southern victories as a sign that he should renew his plan to invade the North. As General Lee moved the Army of Northern Virginia northward, Union Major General George Meade followed him with orders to protect Philadelphia,

Baltimore, and Washington, DC. The two massive armies met in Gettysburg, Pennsylvania, on July 1, 1863.

Figure 8.7: Colonel Joshua Chamberlain

Although the initial battle seemed favorable to the Confederates, they could not dislodge the Union forces. On July 2, reinforcements arrived for both armies, but the Union defenses held. On July 3, General Lee ordered General George E. Pickett, who had just arrived, to make a charge using his 15,000 troops up Cemetery Ridge, where they broke the Union ranks but not at a critical position known as Little Round Top, where the Union counterattack pushed away Pickett's troops. The South could not sustain the territory they had gained and had to withdraw. Colonel Joshua Chamberlain repelled the Confederate attack at Little Round Top using a "swinging gate" bayonet charge. As it turned out, Colonel Chamberlain's maneuver turned the tide in the battle and caused General Lee to abandon his northern assault, which became a major turning point in the Civil War. The casualty figures were indeed staggering: 23,000 Union soldiers and 28,000 Confederate soldiers. Gettysburg was the Civil War's deadliest battle.

The Battle of Vicksburg

From May 22 to July 4, 1863, the North and the South fought at Vicksburg, Mississippi. Controlling Vicksburg would give the Union command of the entire Mississippi River. Vicksburg was heavily defended on a bluff overlooking the river, and General John C. Pemberton commanded the Confederate Forces. General Ulysses S. Grant led his Union forces south to the west side of the Mississippi, passing Vicksburg. Then, he crossed over and attacked the city from the south. By mid-June, General Pemberton was running low on supplies, and on July 4, 1863, he surrendered. The victories at Vicksburg and Gettysburg constituted the turning point of the Civil War. Also, some European powers had considered supporting the South until the North won those two battles.

Two unusual stories from the Battle of Vicksburg feature two animals—an eagle and a camel. The 8th Wisconsin Infantry carried Old Abe, a bald eagle, on a staff as they charged into battle. Old Abe would fly over the battlefield screeching, unnerving the enemy forces. He became the symbol for the screaming eagle on the US Army's 101st Airborne Division patch. On the Confederate side, they had a camel named Old Douglas. He helped carry supplies and maintained morale in several battles, although he often spooked the horses and always refused to be tied up. He was, unfortunately, shot by Union sharpshooters.

New York City Draft Riots

From July 13 to July 16, 1863, White working-class New Yorkers rioted over a new federal draft law requiring that all male citizens between 20 and 35 years old be drafted into the war. For unmarried men, the draft age range extended to 45 years old. Black men were exempted from the draft, so the rioters primarily targeted them in the ensuing violence. Hundreds of people were killed, and many more were injured. The causes of the riots included the fact that wealthy citizens could buy their way out of the draft, Black men were seen as competition for jobs, and many resented the war's emancipation focus after the Emancipation Proclamation. High inflation and high unemployment also added fuel to the fire of discontent.

Gettysburg Address

On November 19, 1863, Lincoln declared "that this nation, under God, shall have a new birth of freedom—and that government of the people, by the people, for the people, shall not perish from the earth." Lincoln viewed the Civil War as completing the American Revolution in his Gettysburg Address. Both the Emancipation Proclamation and the Gettysburg Address set the stage for the inevitable—the end of slavery. Lincoln gave his famous address at the National Cemetery of Gettysburg dedication ceremony. The speech was short, and President Lincoln did not think it went well, but it is considered one of the finest political speeches ever given by a president, and he wrote it himself. His symbolic and powerful words invoked the principles of equality promised in the Declaration of Independence, and his call for a "new birth of freedom" resonated with all Americans, especially those held in bondage.

The Overland Campaign (1864–1865)

President Lincoln placed General Grant in charge of all Union armies with the dual missions of destroying General Johnston's Army of Tennessee and General Lee's Army of Northern Virginia. What became known as General Grant's Overland Campaign included the Battle of the Wilderness, the Battle of Cold Harbor, and the attack on Petersburg. General Grant tirelessly attacked and suffered significant casualties, as did the Confederate forces. General William Tecumseh Sherman was put in charge of the war in the West, where he made his way through Tennessee and northern Georgia, eventually capturing the rail hub in Atlanta by September 1864.

Figure 8.8: General Ulysses S. Grant

The Battle of the Wilderness began on May 5, 1864, and concluded two days later, but then led on to Cold Harbor and Petersburg. The Battle of the Wilderness occurred in the woods near Locust Grove, Virginia, 20 miles west of Fredericksburg. Both armies suffered heavy casualties, almost 99,000 combined. The Battle of the Wilderness did not have a clear winner, but General Grant kept going despite heavy losses. Many have criticized General Grant's war of attrition strategy because of the high casualties, but you cannot argue with his results. General Grant meant to wear down the South and force a surrender.

The Battle of Cold Harbor was fought near Mechanicsville, Virginia, from May 31 to June 12, 1864. General Grant and General Meade were up against General Lee. The Union suffered significant losses (12,738 casualties) and had to withdraw. The South suffered 5,287 total casualties. Despite his devastating loss at Cold Harbor, General Grant was able to cross the James River secretly and continued marching towards Petersburg.

Figure 8.9: Siege Mortar at Petersburg

The Battle of Petersburg, also known as the Siege of Petersburg, took place from June 9, 1864, to March 25, 1865, in Petersburg, Virginia. This siege was a series of battles around Petersburg, the longest in American warfighting history. General Grant, commanding 125,000 Union troops, was again up against General Lee, who commanded around 60,000 soldiers. The Union suffered 42,000 casualties, while the Confederates suffered 28,000 casualties. The siege resulted in a victory for the North. It was not considered a classic military siege because the Union forces dug over 30 miles of trenches, creating the first instance of trench warfare in military history and foreshadowing the First World War. Petersburg was the supply center for the Confederate capital city of Richmond and vital for the continuance of the war for the South. Eventually, General Grant was able to grind down the Confederates, and General Lee was forced to retreat and then surrender at Appomattox Courthouse, Virginia, on April 9, 1865. Oddly, the surrender documents were signed at Wilmer McLean's house, where the war started in 1861 with the First Battle of Bull Run. McLean said, "The war began in my front yard and ended in my front parlor."

The Assassination of President Abraham Lincoln

On April 14, 1865, President Lincoln was assassinated while attending a play entitled *Our American Cousin* at Ford's Theatre in Washington, DC. He was assassinated by a well-known actor and Confederate sympathizer named John Wilkes Booth. Lincoln died the next day from his fatal head wound. He was the first American president to be assassinated. Booth's plot involved others who were to kill Vice President Andrew Johnson and Secretary of State William H. Seward. Seward was only wounded, and Johnson's would-be assassin lost his nerve. John Wilkes Booth jumped from the presidential balcony after he shot Lincoln and yelled to the crowd: "Sic semper tyrannis!" The Latin phrase means "thus be it to tyrants." Booth was killed after a 12-day manhunt, and four others were hanged for their roles in the conspiracy. On an odd note, Lincoln's secretary was named Mrs. Kennedy, and President John F. Kennedy (who was assassinated in 1963) had a secretary named Mrs. Lincoln. The Thirteenth Amendment was ratified on December 6, 1865. "Neither slavery nor involuntary servitude, except as a punishment for crime whereof the party shall have been duly convicted, shall exist within the United States, or any place subject to their jurisdiction." The Thirteenth Amendment completed the abolition of slavery in the United States, which had begun with President Abraham Lincoln issuing the Emancipation Proclamation in 1863.

Conclusion

A counterfactual in history is when you change the outcome of a significant historical event to better understand what would have happened if a different outcome had occurred. For instance, what would have happened had the South won the Civil War? Nobody knows, so it is just speculation, which some historians frown upon (just the facts, ma'am), but I believe it is worthwhile.

1. The country would have stayed split into the United States of America (USA) and the Confederate States of America (CSA).
2. Slavery was becoming less economically viable and would have died out by 1900 or even sooner, perhaps prompting a reunion of North and South.

3. The First World War (the Great War as it was called then) would have led to the CSA and USA allying on different sides and maybe involving Central and South America.

4. The precedent had been set for further secession, and fragmentation could have happened with other regions or states.

5. The South's economy would not have industrialized as quickly and maintained its dependency on agriculture and slave labor.

As interesting as counterfactuals are in exploring critical historical events, developing a more fact-based analysis to compare essential resources for the North and the South is worthwhile. The total White population of the North was 20.28 million, and 5.5 million in the South. There were 435,000 African Americans in the North and 3.65 million in the South. The total number of draft-eligible (15–30 years old) White males in the North was 2.58 million as opposed to 791,000 in the South. There were 110,000 factories in the North and only 18,000 in the South. The North had 1.3 million industrial workers, whereas the South only had 110,000. The Union had 451 steam locomotives, and the Confederacy had just 19 locomotives. In 1860, the North had 21,973 miles of railroad track instead of only 9,283 in the South. The North had many more resources and greater strength to start with. Maybe a better question is why the North took so long to win. The answer is that the Union knew they had such an abundance of resources, leading them to devise a less lean and resource-efficient strategy than the Confederacy. In other words, the North often squandered its resources, which led to a higher death toll and the war dragging on longer than it could have. I think that might have been more important than the reason some historians give that the South had better generals. There were great military leaders on both sides.

Another question that needs to be answered is why poor Southerners fought to preserve slavery when they did not own any slaves. One likely reason is that the slave economy produced fabulous wealth, with the Southern states having a higher per capita income than the North. The wealth trickled down, or so they thought. Also, with slaves inhabiting the lowest rung of the economic ladder, poor White people felt that at least they were not at the bottom. The truth was that even after the Civil War ended and slavery was abolished, the wealthiest Southerners retained their wealth and stature, whereas the poor suffered. However, Civil War author and historian Shelby Foote probably provided the most immediate and straightforward answer. He noted that when Confederate soldiers were asked why they were fighting, they would say: "Because y'all are down here." Foote also indicated that one must understand the Civil War to understand America. In many ways, the Civil War completed the American Revolution. President Lincoln said in the Gettysburg

Address that it was "a new birth of freedom." Foote correctly asserted that "the Civil War made us, an is." Before the Civil War, it was common to refer to the United States in the plural: "The United States are a nice place to live." After the Civil War, it was customary to refer to the United States in the singular: "The United States is a nice place to live." That simple change carries a lot of meaning, namely that the Civil War made us one nation.

When the last shots were fired in 1865, the Union was restored, and slavery abolished, there was still much work to be done to heal the nation. What status would former slaves have in society? What would plantation owners do with their land but no labor? What would former slaves do with their labor but no land to work? Black people faced legal problems and a world that was still stratified by race. Without Abraham Lincoln to guide them, Americans faced the daunting task of reconstructing the nation.

Credits

Figure 8.1: Abraham Lincoln. Source: https://commons.wikimedia.org/wiki/File:Abraham_Lincoln_head_on_shoulders_photo_portrait.jpg

Figure 8.2: The First Battle of Bull Run. Source: https://ahec.armywarcollege.edu/exhibits/CivilWarImagery/images/1861Vol%209%20Pg%20450%20Bull%20Run%20Litho.jpg

Figure 8.3: The Battle of Shiloh. Source: https://images.mohistory.org/images/N20994_0001/original.jpg

Figure 8.4: General Robert E. Lee. Source: https://commons.wikimedia.org/wiki/File:Robert_Edward_Lee.jpg

Figure 8.5: Battle of the Ironclads. Source: https://commons.wikimedia.org/wiki/File:Ironclads_battle_7.jpg

Figure 8.6: The Storming of Fort Wagner. Source: https://commons.wikimedia.org/wiki/File:The_Storming_of_Ft_Wagner-lithograph_by_Kurz_and_Allison_1890.jpg

Figure 8.7: Colonel Joshua Chamberlain. Source: https://loc.gov/pictures/resource/cwpbh.03163/

Figure 8.8: General Ulysses S. Grant. Source: https://mohistory.org/collections/item/N27765

Figure 8.9: Siege Mortar at Petersburg. Source: https://commons.wikimedia.org/wiki/File:Dictatorcrop.jpg

Recommended Sources

Civil War Photographs. https://www.loc.gov/pictures/search/?st=grid&co=cwp

Shelby Foote. *The Civil War: A Narrative.* In three volumes.

Civil War Battlefields. https://www.battlefields.org/civil-war-related-websites

CONCLUSION

Claiming America

"Those who deny freedom to others deserve it not for themselves, and, under a just God, cannot long retain it."

—*Abraham Lincoln*

They say the best way to learn something is to try teaching it. I would subscribe to that and add this slight modification: "The best way to learn a subject is to try to teach the subject or write a book about it or both." I have taught early and modern US history for over 33 years. I have learned much from my students as their questions guide me into nuances and nooks and crannies of American history that I might not have explored without their prompting me to do so. In writing this book, I dove deep into the early period of American history that I had not explored before, at least not so extensively, because my main field was modern US history. I believe I have become a better teacher as a result. We will know for sure when I present this book to my students.

We are again at a crossroads, dear readers, where the country is divided along many fault lines, and few are willing to compromise or listen to the other side. Such was the period before the Civil War. I fear that we have all the prerequisites in place for another one. It will be up to you to follow Abraham Lincoln's advice and listen to the "better angels of our nature." Both sides in the political divide in America accuse the other side of being an existential threat. Those apocalyptic terms leave little room for compromise. I often think of the age-old problem: do the means justify the ends? In other words, if the other side is an existential threat, does that justify using any means necessary to defeat them?

We have come full circle. In an age of cancel culture, division, scorn, and hatred, we cannot give in to the idea that we must silence those with whom we disagree to save democracy. Hyperbolic rhetoric is dangerous. If you do succumb to such partisan dogma, sooner or later, they will come for you. That is why freedom of speech is a part of the First Amendment. My America is your America and is our America, my dear reader, from sea to shining sea, as they say. The Civil War made us one nation but left us with many questions. From a group of disparate religious dissenters, farmers, laborers, soldiers, explorers, missionaries, Indigenous people, enslaved Africans, indentured servants, and many others, we somehow survived the Civil War. We were poised to take on the world through rapid industrialization as one nation, imperfect but with promise. The preamble to the US Constitution states:

"We the people of the United States, in order to form a more perfect union, establish justice, insure domestic tranquility, provide for the common defense, promote the general welfare, and secure the blessings of liberty to ourselves and our posterity, do ordain and establish this Constitution for the United States of America."

The words and phrases are striking and promise hope for a perfect society. The word "more" allows for improvement. And so, we continue to work on our union, like a married couple that struggles through their early years of marriage, facing trials and tribulations and hoping they can survive against the odds to stay together for the rest of their lives. It is hard not to shed a tear when you hear about a couple who have been married for 50 years (like my parents) or even those who have made it for 75 years. How did they make it? They resisted the urge to throw everything away and abandon ship by dwelling on the bad times, the grievances, the arguments, and the pain, and realized that no matter who you are or who you are with, there will be all those things. If couples are lucky, they will stick it out to find domestic tranquility and live together in harmony. That is the hope because, as President John F. Kennedy said: "Our most basic common link is that we all inhabit this planet. We all breathe the same air. We all cherish our children's future. And we are all mortal." This is my America, this is your America, and this is our America. In the words of folk singer Woody Guthrie:

This land is your land,
this land is my land
From California,
to the New York Island
From the redwood forest,
to the gulf stream waters
This land was made for you and me.

Figure C-1: Woody Guthrie
Source: https://commons.wikimedia.org/wiki/File:Woody_Guthrie_NYWTS.jpg

Index

Abolitionism, 137
Abraham Lincoln, 80, 110, 128, 142, 145, 146, 148, 154, 159, 161, 163
Alexander Hamilton, 84, 86, 90, 91, 92, 93, 95, 104, 105, 147
Álvar Núñez Cabeza de Vaca, 32, 33, 38
American Civil War, 2, 84, 117, 134, 146
American Revolution, 63, 64, 65, 67, 68, 75, 76, 77, 79, 80, 81, 83, 95, 100, 119, 141, 145, 156, 160
American Revolutionary War, 41, 64, 75, 94
Amerigo Vespucci, 36
Andrew Jackson, 116, 117
Ann Hutchinson, 44, 45, 60
Annapolis Convention, 84
Anti-Federalist, 68, 90
Appomattox, 147, 159
Articles of Confederation, 77, 84, 85, 86
Bacon's Rebellion, 53, 54
Barrow, 10, 11, 13
Battle at Antietam, 149
Battle of Gettysburg, 154
Battle of Ironclads, 150
Battle of New Orleans, 116
Battle of Shiloh, 149, 161
Benjamin Franklin, 69, 73, 74, 85, 89, 138, 147
Bering Sea Land Bridge, 6, 38
Bill of Rights, 80, 83, 86, 88, 90, 147
Bleeding Kansas, 133
Boston Massacre, 66, 70
Brigham Young, 134
Bull Run, 148, 159, 161
California Gold Rush, 131, 135
Chief Kamiakin, 20, 21
Christopher Columbus, 5, 6, 27, 31
Citizen Edmond-Charles Genêt, 94

Civil War, 84, 104, 108, 110, 120, 121, 123, 125, 127, 129, 137, 138, 142, 145, 146, 147, 149, 150, 151, 153, 154, 155, 156, 159, 160, 162, 163
Coercive Acts, 70
Colonel Bill Wenger, 75
Columbian Exchange, 5, 27, 36, 37, 38
Confederate, 145, 146, 147, 148, 149, 150, 151, 152, 153, 154, 155, 156, 157, 159, 160
Connecticut, 41, 43, 53, 54, 55, 56, 85, 87
Constitutional Convention, 84, 85, 87, 89
Continental Army, 69, 72, 73, 74, 84
Continental Congress, 69, 71, 72
cotton gin, 109, 113
Daniel Shays, 84, 85, 104
Dartmouth v. Woodward, 109
David Willson, 14
Declaration of Independence, 68, 77, 83, 95, 98, 125, 138, 157
Declaratory Act, 66
Delaware, 41, 52, 57, 73, 74, 81, 84, 86, 87
Dred Scott, 138, 139, 143
Dutch East India Company, 34
Eli Whitney, 109
Elizabeth Cady Stanton, 125
Emancipation Proclamation, 110, 147, 151, 152, 156, 159
England, 31, 34, 35, 41, 42, 43, 44, 46, 48, 52, 53, 54, 55, 56, 57, 60, 64, 65, 66, 67, 68, 70, 71, 72, 73, 75, 76, 77, 80, 83, 89, 90, 93, 94, 100, 101, 103, 107, 114, 124, 129, 135
Erie Canal, 108, 109, 121
Federalist, 68, 80, 84, 85, 86, 92, 95, 96, 97
Fort Sumter, 145, 146, 147

Founding Fathers, 63, 67, 68, 76, 77, 80, 97, 138, 147
Fox sisters, 127, 128, 129
France, 31, 35, 41, 43, 64, 65, 74, 75, 76, 80, 90, 93, 94, 98, 100, 107
Francisco Pizarro, 31, 32
Frederick Douglass, 139, 140, 141, 152, 154
French and Indian War, 41, 64, 65, 66, 69
French Revolution, 63, 80, 94, 107
Fugitive Slave Law, 138, 145
General Charles Cornwallis, 74
George Washington, 1, 64, 69, 72, 76, 85, 86, 87, 88, 90, 92, 98, 105, 113, 147
Georgia, 41, 42, 52, 57, 71, 87, 118, 119, 157
Gettysburg Address, 156, 161
Great Awakening, 67, 123
Great Britain, 34, 41, 43, 52, 57, 60, 63, 65, 66, 68, 71, 73, 74, 76, 90, 93, 95, 99, 100, 101
Great Lakes, 14, 36, 86, 100, 108, 109, 118
Henry David Thoreau, 43, 136
Henry Hudson, 34
Hernán Cortés, 31, 32
Hopi, 7, 17, 18
Indian Removal Act, 117, 119
indigo, 52, 57
Inupiat, 7, 10, 11, 12, 13
Jacksonian Democracy, 116
Jacques Cartier, 36
James K. Polk, 132
James Madison, 84, 86, 88, 89, 90, 95, 96, 101, 105, 147
Jamestown, 34, 41, 42, 52
Jefferson Davis, 147
Jeffersonian Democracy, 97, 116
JoAllyn Archambault, 5
John Adams, 64, 65, 66, 72, 73, 80, 81, 90, 94, 96, 147
John Brown, 140, 141, 143

John Hancock, 70, 72
John Jay, 86, 93
John Quincy Adams, 116
John Wilkes Booth, 80, 159
John Winthrop, 44, 45, 56
Joseph Smith, 134
Joshua Chamberlain, 154, 155, 161
Juneteenth, 110, 152
Ken Burns, 5
Kenneth Arnold, 24
King George III, 65
King Philip's War, 54, 55
La Isabela, 32
Leif Erikson, 6, 25, 27, 38
Lewis and Clark, 98, 99, 104, 105, 129
Lexington and Concord, 72, 73
Louisiana Purchase, 90, 98, 99, 129, 132
Louisiana Territory, 90
Lucas Vázquez de Ayllón, 42
Lucretia Mott, 124, 125, 137, 142
Major General Gordon Granger, 110
Manifest Destiny, 116, 117, 129
Margaret Fuller, 136, 142
Martin Luther, 19, 44
Mary Todd Lincoln, 128, 129, 142
Maryland, 41, 52, 53, 55, 57, 86, 87, 107, 108, 140, 149
Mason-Dixon line, 86
Massachusetts, 35, 41, 43, 44, 46, 54, 55, 56, 70, 72, 73, 84, 87, 94, 95, 114, 115, 125, 136, 152
Massachusetts Bay, 35, 44, 46, 54
Mayflower, 35
Mexican-American War, 108, 133, 135
Middle Colonies, 52, 53, 57, 67, 72, 76
Minutemen, 72
Mississippi River, 14, 65, 86, 98, 109, 134, 156
Missouri Compromise, 130, 132, 138
Mormon, 134
Mormons, 134
Mount Adams, 21, 24

Nat Turner, 110, 111, 121, 138
Nathaniel Bacon, 53, 54
Netherlands, 31, 33, 34, 43, 52, 74
New England, 43, 44, 53, 55, 57, 66, 114
New Hampshire, 41, 43, 46, 56, 87
New Jersey, 41, 52, 57, 73, 84, 85, 87
New London, 46, 49, 51
New York, 25, 34, 35, 36, 38, 41, 49, 52, 55, 57, 70, 73, 74, 84, 108, 109, 115, 125, 127, 128, 134, 156, 164
North Carolina, 34, 41, 52, 75, 109, 118
Northwest Territory, 86, 93, 102
Nullification Crisis, 117, 147
Oregon Trail, 130, 131, 142
Patrick Henry, 63, 77, 79, 80, 86, 147
Pennsylvania, 41, 52, 55, 57, 84, 86, 87, 92, 138, 149, 155
Pequot War, 54, 55
Phil Red Eagle, 14, 15, 16
Pilgrims, 35, 38, 44
Plymouth, 35, 38, 44, 46, 54, 55
Pocahontas, 34
Portugal, 31, 36, 43, 57
Puritans, 35, 43, 44, 46, 55, 57
railway, 20, 108, 109, 149
Ralph Waldo Emerson, 43, 136
Republican Party, 92, 121
Rhode Island, 41, 43, 45, 53, 55, 57, 85, 87, 113
rice, 37, 52, 53
Richard Henry Lee, 72, 73, 84, 147
Roanoke Colony, 34
Robert E. Lee, 140, 149, 150, 154, 161
Sacajawea, 98, 99, 105
Salem, 55, 56, 60
Samuel Adams, 70, 72, 147
Samuel de Champlain, 36
Saratoga, 74
Seneca Falls Convention, 125, 127, 128, 135
Sequoyah, 119
Seven Years' War, 64, 65

Shays' Rebellion, 84, 92, 94
Sioux, 7, 14
Sir Walter Raleigh, 34
slavery, 37, 38, 41, 42, 43, 54, 55, 57, 58, 60, 68, 76, 77, 84, 86, 90, 97, 98, 100, 109, 110, 111, 119, 120, 123, 124, 125, 127, 130, 132, 133, 135, 136, 137, 138, 139, 140, 141, 145, 146, 147, 148, 151, 153, 156, 159, 160, 161
smallpox, 37, 38, 131
South Carolina, 41, 42, 52, 57, 72, 87, 95, 117, 118, 145, 147, 152
Southern Colonies, 52, 53, 57, 76
Spain, 31, 32, 33, 37, 41, 43, 57, 65, 74, 99
Spiritualism, 125, 127, 128, 129, 135, 142
State's Rights, 147
sugar, 10, 36, 37, 58, 59, 131
Sugar Act, 66
Susquehannock War, 54, 55
The Articles of Confederation, 69, 83, 84
The Civil War, 142
The Constitution, 86
The Mexican-American War, 132, 133, 142
The Stamp Act, 60, 66
The Treaty of Paris, 83
The Virginia Plan, 85
The War of 1812, 100, 103, 104
Thomas Banyacya, 17, 18
Thomas Jefferson, 66, 72, 73, 84, 86, 90, 91, 95, 96, 97, 98, 99, 101, 105, 109, 110, 129, 138, 147
Thomas Paine, 72, 80, 147
tobacco, 34, 37, 52, 53, 54, 57, 107, 109
Trail of Tears, 118, 119, 120, 121
transatlantic slave trade, 36, 58
Transcendentalism, 135
Ulysses S. Grant, 133, 149, 156, 157, 161

Uncle Tom's Cabin, 139
Union, 20, 115, 117, 133, 145, 146, 147, 148, 149, 150, 151, 154, 155, 156, 157, 158, 160, 161
Valley Forge, 69, 75
Vicksburg, 156
Vinland, 27
Virginia, 34, 41, 42, 44, 52, 53, 54, 57, 64, 67, 72, 74, 79, 80, 81, 84, 85, 86, 97, 109, 110, 118, 138, 140, 147, 148, 150, 154, 157, 158
Virginia Company, 34, 42, 52
Werner Herzog, 2
Whiskey Rebellion, 92, 93, 94, 104, 105
Whitman Massacre, 131
William Bradford, 35, 56
William Lloyd Garrison, 137, 138, 139
William Mumler, 129
William Penn, 52, 57
XYZ Affair, 94
Yakama, 7, 20, 21, 23
Yorktown, 69, 74

About the Author

Bruce Olav Solheim was born in Seattle, Washington, to Norwegian immigrant parents. A disabled veteran, he served for six years in the US Army as a jail guard in West Germany, and later as a warrant officer helicopter pilot at the 82nd Airborne Division. As a civilian, Solheim worked as a defense contractor at Boeing for five years, then went on to earn his Ph.D. in history from Bowling Green State University in 1993, with his main field being US foreign policy. Bruce was the first person in his family to go to college and is currently a distinguished professor of history at Citrus College in Glendora, California, where he has taught for 26 years. As a Fulbright Professor and Scholar, Dr. Solheim taught at the University of Tromsø in northern Norway in 2003.

In 2001, Dr. Solheim founded the veterans' program at Citrus College and, in 2007, co-founded (along with Ginger De Villa-Rose and former East Los Angeles Vet Center Director Manuel Martinez) the first in the nation college transition course for recently returned veterans called Boots to Books.

A prolific writer, Solheim has published twelve books and written ten plays, six of which have been produced. In addition to his academic books/journal/novel *(The Nordic Nexus: A Lesson in Peaceful Security, On Top of the World: Women's Political Leadership in Scandinavia and Beyond, Viet Nam Generation Journal, Women in Power: World Leaders since 1960, The Vietnam War Era: A Personal Journey, Ali's Bees, Making History: A Personal Approach to Modern American History, and I'm An American: A Personal Approach to Early American History)*, he has published several books about the paranormal. In fact, Dr. Solheim teaches a Paranormal Personal History course at Citrus College.

Alongside his list of published works, Solheim has also published two comic book series. *Snarc* (issues 1 and 2) features an alien hybrid character of the same name, and *Dr. Jekyll Alien Hunter* (issues 1 and 2) with a female lead character. He's working on a third comic book called *Gig Line*, an autobiographical graphic novel. Bruce is married to Ginger and has four children (one serving in the US Air Force) and two grandsons.